Songs From A Golden Age
Parlour Songs Arranged for Classical/Fingerstyle Guitar and Voice

Arranged by Adrian Allan
Edited by Allan H. Jones

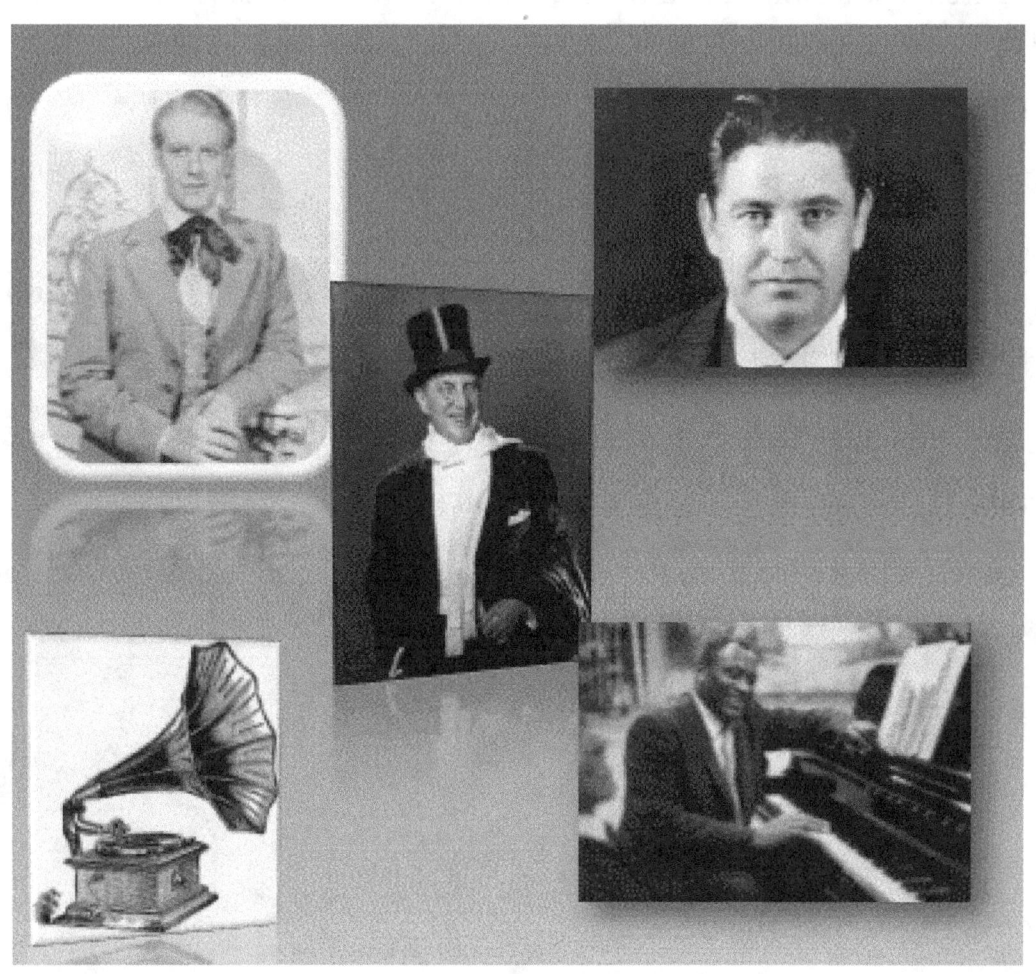

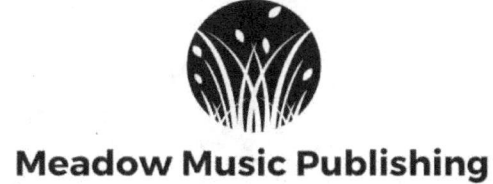

Meadow Music Publishing

First Edition: 2018

ISBN: 978-0-244-9954-1

Meadow Music Publishing
23c Burford Rd
Manchester, M16 8EW

adrianallan12345@gmail.com

www.facebook.com/meadowmusicpublishing/

Front cover: Clockwise from top left: Nelson Eddy; John McCormack; Paul Robeson; Victor Victrola Phonograph. Centre: Richard Tauber.

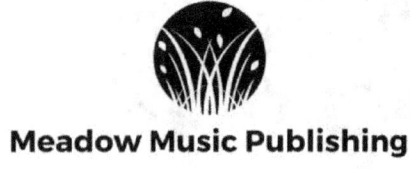

Meadow Music Publishing

Contents

Preface

The songs in the current volume were selected to represent the very best examples of the genre of the *parlour song*. They have been arranged for guitar and voice from the original piano-vocal editions. In the interests of authenticity, all of the original markings for tempo, dynamics and expression are exactly the same as on the original song-sheet. It was the norm to produce the songs in multiple keys to suit the range of the vocalist. In this book, guitar-friendly key signatures have been chosen; avoiding multiple flats. A vocal range is offered that can be performed by the majority of singers - all of the songs sit within the range of G below middle C, to the E on the top space of the staff, with the exception of a solitary high F in *Roses of Picardy*. Male singers will perform the songs an octave below this range.

The piano allows up to ten notes to be played simultaneously, the guitar only six (if strummed), or four if plucked. The aim was to, wherever possible, reproduce the original piano accompaniment – the emphasis being on *transcription* rather than *arrangement*. Compromises have been made to the often thick chordal texture of these songs. However, the general harmonic intent has been maintained. Chords have generally been kept in the same inversion bass-lines have been maintained wherever possible. The exact voicings have been adapted to suit the idiomatic nature of the guitar. The guitarist may want to simplify further still – these arrangements act as a reasonably authentic starting point for a performance.

Attention has been paid within this book to the popular exponents of parlour singing. John McCormack perhaps provides the most authentic insight into contemporary performance practice; we are fortunate that his career coincided with the earliest examples of recorded sound. His vocal delivery is powerful, but not overwhelming – he found his niche as a lyric tenor, rather than a dramatic tenor in the manner of Caruso. Parlour songs are frequently embellished with expressive rubato, and a number of the pieces call for the accompanist to follow the melodic rhythm set by the vocalist at key points in the performance – *colla voce*.

Parlour Songs – A Brief History: The name parlour song comes from the room in which middle class families in the Victorian and Edwardian period entertained visitors and displayed their best furniture. No respectable home was complete without a piano, and it was a staple of domestic entertainment before the invention of the gramophone and recorded sound. Song-sheets were items of mass consumption, and popular songs of the day could sell over a million copies. A customer visiting a music shop would ask the shop's resident performer to play the piece before deciding to purchase the sheet music.

Parlour ballads are replete with references to the Victorian middle class themes of domesticity, family life and a love of nature. Their musical structure is often quite sophisticated and unlike contemporaneous music hall songs, parlour songs make frequent use of chromatic harmonies and altered chords. Their musical value is the main reason why these songs have stood the test of time, and are still frequently performed by operatic "cross-over" artists whose repertoire is chosen from both classical music and popular song.

Popular Recording Artists of Parlour Songs:

Richard Tauber (1891-1948) Richard Tauber was one of the most revered tenors of the early twentieth century. Born in Linz, Austria, he made his public debut in 1912 and in 1922 signed a five-year contract with the Vienna State Opera where he specialised in performances of Mozart's operas. Tauber gravitated towards operetta from the 1920s and worked closely with Franz Lehar. He made his London debut in 1938 and resided in England after the German annexation of Austria. Apart from his performances of opera and operetta, he left a rich legacy of recordings of popular songs of the day, including many parlour songs and ballads. Richard Tauber recorded all of the songs in this collection, and they can be readily listened to on *Youtube*.

Paul Robeson (1898-1976) Paul Robeson was an American bass-baritone who was also well known for stage and film roles. From the 1920s onwards Robeson recorded hundreds of songs covering a wide range of genres, from popular standards, classical music and parlour songs. In 1928 he landed the part of Joe from *Showboat* at the Theatre Royal, Drury Lane. As time progressed, Robeson became more deeply embroiled in political activism, including trade unionism and the Civil Rights movement; in 1952 he was awarded the International Stalin Award by the Soviet Union and was subsequently subjected to close political scrutiny by the American secret services. Robeson recorded *Sylvia, At Dawning, A Perfect Day* and *Trees* in this collection.

John McCormack (1884-1945) John McCormack was born in Athlone, County Westmeath in 1884. In 1905 he travelled to Milan to study with Vincenzo Sabatini, and made his operatic debut in 1906. His breath control was legendary; he could perform 64 notes in one breath in the aria *Il Me Tesoro* from Mozart's *Don Giovanni*. Early in his career McCormack decided to focus on concert performances accompanied by a pianist. His early recordings were made on a phonograph cylinder from 1904 and he continued to record until 1942. McCormack achieved enormous popular success with the song *I Hear You Calling Me*, which became his signature tune. He ended his performing career in 1938, with a performance at the Royal Albert Hall. John McCormack recorded the songs *I Hear You Calling Me, Roses Of Picardy, Sylvia,* Trees, *Kashmiri Love Song* and *At Dawning* in this collection.

Nelson Eddy (1901-1967) Nelson Eddy was a classically trained baritone who starred in 19 films, as well as being a popular recording artist and radio performer. Eddy developed his singing while he was a chorister in church choirs. By the late 1920s he performed with Philadelphia Civic Opera Society and has a repertoire of 28 operas. Eddy was discovered by Hollywood in the 1930s and signed a contract with Metro-Goldwyn-Mayer (MGM). He became associated with Jeanette MacDonald, with whom he shared the main role in many films, most notably, Rose Marie in 1936. Eddy made more than 290 recordings between 1935 and 1964 and made over 600 radio appearances. He recorded *Sylvia, Kashmiri Love Song, A Perfect Day, Trees,* and *At Dawning* in this collection.

Other Notable Performers of Parlour Songs

 Peter Dawson. Australian bass-baritone (1882-1961)

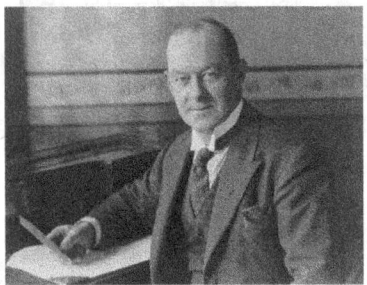 Richard Crooks. American baritone (1900-1972)

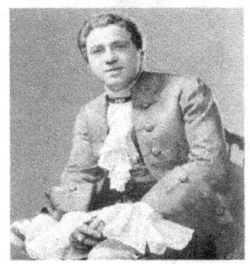 Stuart Burrows. Welsh tenor (b.1933)

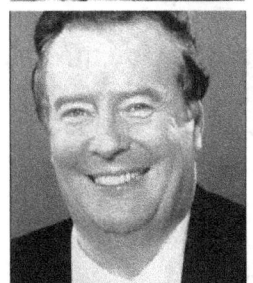 Robert White. American tenor (b.1936)

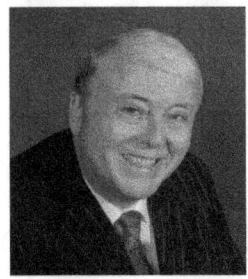 Benjamin Luxon. British baritone (b.1937)

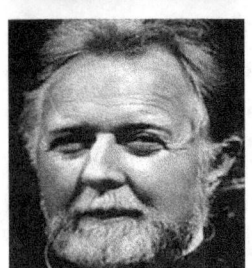 Robert Tear. Welsh baritone (1939-2011)

Sound Recording in the Era of Parlour Songs

Thomas Edison invented the phonograph in 1877, which was basically a sheet of tinfoil wrapped around a cylindrical drum which, when turned by a handle, a stylus embossed a groove in the tinfoil to reflect the pressure variations of the recorded sound. Ten years after this, a wax cylinder phonograph was developed. A hard-wax removable cylinder replaced the soft tinfoil-covered fixed drum. At first, the cylinders could only be played a few dozen times before the grooves wore out.

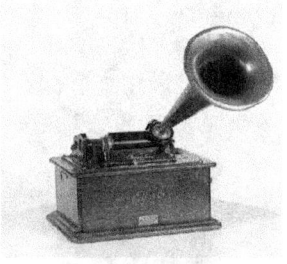

Edison Wax Cylinder Phonograph

In 1902 Edison Records launched a line of improved hard wax cylinders marketed as "Edison Gold Molded Records. An alternative to the cylinder, the 'gramophone' emerged between 1887 and 1893. The stylus moved across disc and recorded on it by causing a stylus attached to a vibrating diaphragm to cut a groove in a lateral plane (from side to side) rather than the vertical plane used by cylinders.

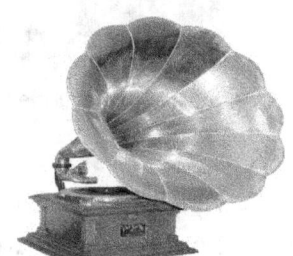

Early Victor Gramophone

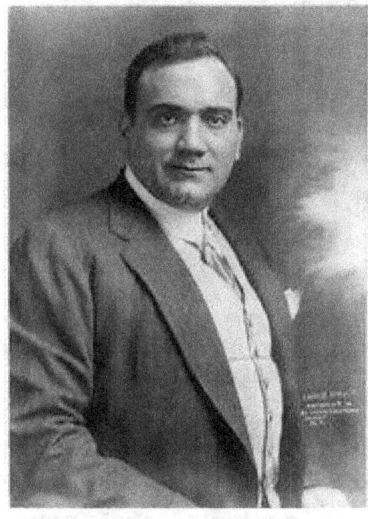

Enrico Caruso (1873-1921)

These earliest recordings tended to be those of celebrity opera singers, such as Enrico Caruso, whose first recordings took place around the turn of the twentieth century. John McCormack followed soon afterwards, from 1904-6, and his early recordings include a mixture of operatic arias, folk songs and parlour songs. McCormack recorded *I Hear You Calling Me* twice for Odeon starting in 1908 and a further four times for Victor between 1910 and 1927. He recorded *Roses of Picardy* in 1919.

Until 1925, recordings had been "acoustic" - a large conical horn was used to focus the air pressure of the sound waves. These early recordings were of low fidelity audible sound spectrum — typically only from around 250 Hz up to about 2,500 Hz, although humans can hear from around 20- 20,000 Hz.

However, it is still fascinating to hear early recordings of parlour songs by artists such as John McCormack, and to gain an insight into how they were performed well over a century ago. Attempts to reduce surface noise and to digitally enhance these early recordings are ongoing – a new complete edition of the recordings of John McCormack is scheduled for release in late-2018.

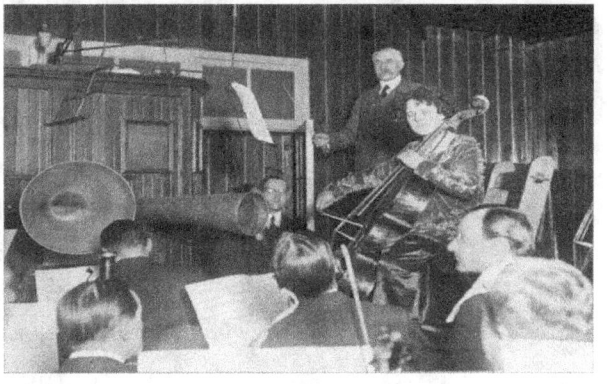

An acoustic recording of Elgar's
Cello Concerto, directed by the composer

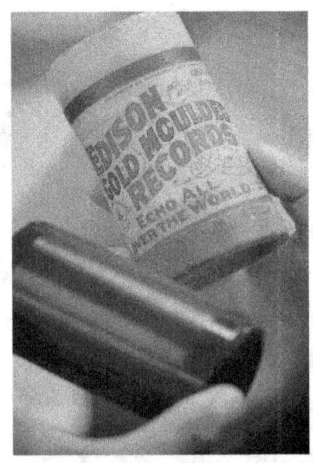

The painstaking process employed by the sound engineer Ward Marston involves sourcing the best possible examples of the recorded artefacts by McCormack, on cylinder or disc, from collectors around the world. Marston makes use of a range of styluses, some of which provide improved sound fidelity. From that point, research is undertaken to correct the pitch of the recording, based on contemporary accounts of the key signature that McCormack chose for each song. Technology is used to isolate a repress disc surface noise and to expand the frequency range to provide an improved listening experience before the recordings are transferred to a digital medium.

Edison wax cylinder and case

Nelson Eddy, Richard Tauber and Paul Robeson had careers that focussed on the electrical era of sound recordings - electrical microphones, electronic signal amplifiers and electromechanical recorders. Sound could now be captured, amplified, filtered and balanced electronically and replayed through an electric-acoustic loudspeaker. The recordings from this era (and the later recordings of McCormack) are inevitably

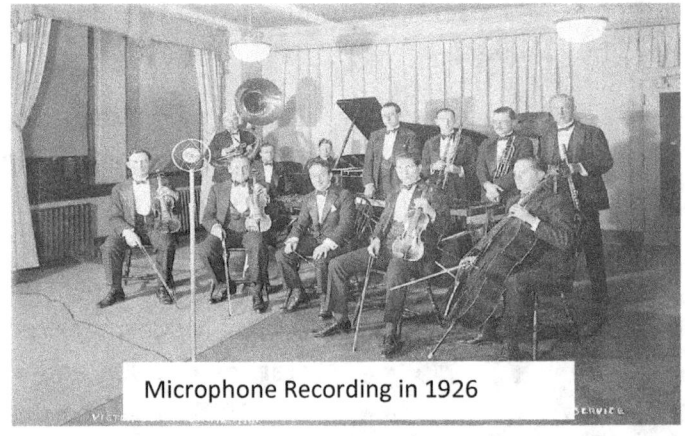

Microphone Recording in 1926

much better in quality, possessing a fidelity across a much wider range of the acoustic spectrum.

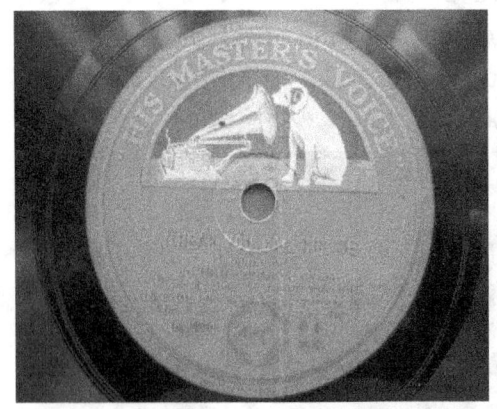

The label of a 78 pressing of McCormack's "I Hear You Calling Me"

However, the electrical era was a double-edged sword; the need to project the voice across large concert halls was solved by invention of the microphone. In its wake a new era of singers replaced the quasi-operatic style of vocalists from the beginning of the century. For example, Bing Crosby, who was more reliant on the microphone and sang in a softer, more personal style, found fame in America and across Europe. By the 1950s, styles had changed to the extent that it must have been hard to contemplate that singers like John McCormack and Richard Tauber had once been global musical superstars, and had dominated the airwaves and filled concert halls in the earlier part of the century.

Songs In This Volume:

Roses of Picardy was composed by Haydn Wood in 1916, with the lyrics supplied by Frederick Weatherley, an English lawyer, author, lyricist and broadcaster. Picardy was a historical province of France which contained the Somme battlefields – the scene of some of the fiercest fighting during the First World War. The song became popular throughout Britain and the US. British soldiers singing it when they enlisted for the Front in France and Flanders. During the First World War, the song sold at a rate of 50,000 copies of the sheet music per month, earning Haydn Wood approximately £10,000 in total (£447,055 in 2018 adjusted for inflation). Following the war, the singing of the song reportedly helped soldiers who were suffering from shell shock to regain their powers of speech. There were three editions of the song published; in Bb ("low"), C ("medium") and D ("high"). The most commonly found edition is in C, and has been used as the basis for this arrangement.

Sylvia was written by the American songwriter Oley Speaks (1874-1948) in 1914. He also wrote many religious songs, as well as *On The Road To Mandalay*, based on a poem by Rudyard Kipling. The lyrics for Sylvia, penned by Clinton Schollard, are rich in similes which conflate the subject of the poem with an assortment of natural features, "And the touch of Sylvia's hand is as light as milk weed down". The song features an extended tonic pedal note across several bars, in this case, a dropped D note on string 6.

Trees (1922) by Oscar Rasbach (1888-1975) is based on a lyric poem by American poet Joyce Kilmer that perceives as the inability of art created by humankind to replicate the beauty achieved by nature. The song was performed by many great singers, including Nelson Eddy, Robert Merrill, and Paul Robeson. In bar 5, an alternative (*ossia*) passage has been offered, for those who find it hard to lift a barre to leave the e string free to ring. The same passage is encountered at bar 18.

A Perfect Day was composed by the American songwriter Carrie Jacobs-Bond in 1909. It was phenomenally successful, and the sheet music sold over five million copies. Jacobs-Bond was also an accomplished artist; she illustrated the covers of her song book collections. A Perfect Day became her most requested song when she entertained troops at U.S. Army camps during the First World War. This arrangement remains quite faithful to the original piano version. As such, it does present some right hand challenges, and most bars are split into three voices. With careful practice and attention to fingering, a legato effect can be achieved on the guitar.

At Dawning was written in 1906 by the American songwriter Charles Wakefield Cadman. He was also an authority on the music of American Indians and tribal instruments. In this arrangement, the sixth string is dropped to D. This is the only song in the collection in 3/4 time. It is also probably the most romantically inspired, featuring a persistent repetition of the phrase, "I love you". The textual instruction of *con molta espress* right at the start of the song, as well as the *affetuoso* at bar 16 ("with tender and passionate expression"), further reinforces this view.

I Hear You Calling Me was a British popular song published in London in 1908. The lyrics were by Harold Lake (a journalist writing as Harold Harford) and the music by Charles Marshall. The song became a bestseller for the tenor John McCormack - it was his signature piece, and was recorded six times during his life. The words are particularly poignant- it concerns hearing the sound of a loved one's voice from beyond the grave. The song was based on the story of 16-year-old pupil at an elementary school in Canterbury who met a girl nearly a year his junior. Sadly the girl died of consumption (what is now known as tuberculosis) three years later.

Kashmiri Song (Pale Hands I Loved). This was one of the most popular songs at the turn of the twentieth century (written in 1902) and remained so until the Second World War. The song, written by Amy Woodforde-Finden was based on a poem by Laurence Hope (pseudonym of Adela Florence Nicolson) and was taken from a collection called *India's Love Lyrics*. *The Shalimar* mentioned in the lyrics probably refers to either the Shalimar Gardens in Kashmir or Lahore. The appeal of the song, as well as longevity, probably lies in its colourful and sometimes exotic harmonies, which are a perfect match for the subject matter of the song.

Until. Wilfred Sanderson (1878 – 1935) was a composer and organist based in Doncaster. He studied organ under Frederick Bridge as a pupil and later assistant organist at Westminster Abbey from 1895 - 1904. During this time, Wilfrid was present during Queen Victoria's funeral and memorial service held on 2 February 1901. He wrote around 170 songs, and also some pieces for piano and organ. His most famous song was *Until* – its sheet music sold over a million copies. The guitar arrangement in this volume uses a dropped D tuning on string 6. There are a number of challenging voicings and stretches in the guitar part, which make it one of the more difficult pieces in the book. The original piano score contains breathing marks, which are reproduced here. Another point of interest is bars 11 and 14; alternative notes are suggested in the score, presented here as cue-sized note-heads. The glissando in bar 3 has been added as a guitar-specific effect to aid the melodic shift from C# to the bass note of B.

Tempo Suggestions

Tempo markings for these songs can be misleading. For example, A Perfect Day is marked *moderato espressivo*, which might suggest a tempo slightly slower than *moderato*. However, it is normally performed around crotchet=70, which is more in line with *adagio*. The following tempo markings (BPM) are suggestions based on performance practice:

Roses Of Picardy: 100-110	*Sylvia: 80-90*	*Trees: 65-70*
A Perfect Day: 70	*At Dawning: 60-70*	*I Hear You Calling Me: 80-90*
Kashmiri Song (Pale Hands I Loved): 60-70		*Until: 60-70*

Roses Of Picardy

Fred E Weatherley

Hayden Wood

Brightly *(Almost two beats in a bar)*

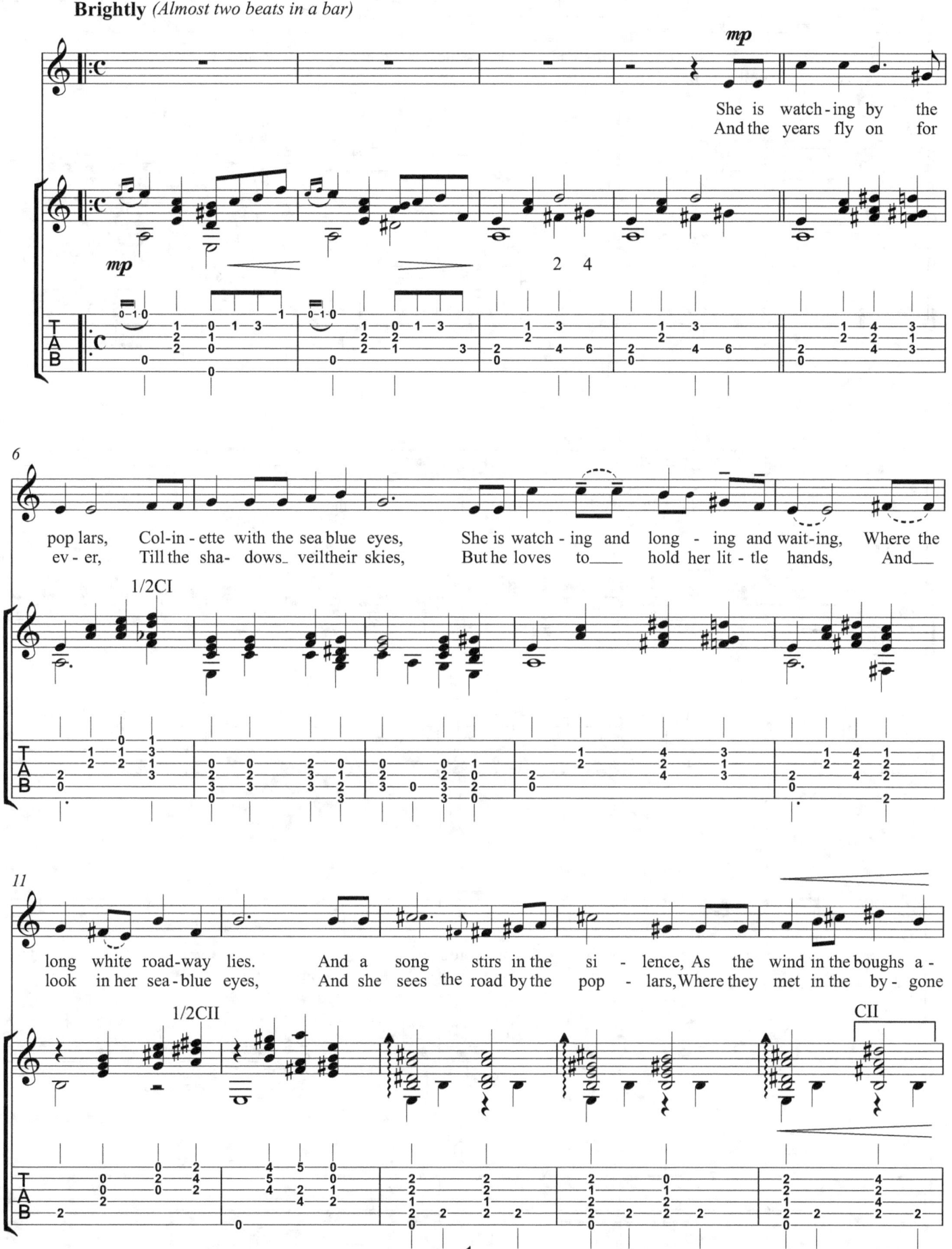

She is watch-ing by the
And the years fly on for

pop lars,   Col-in-ette with the sea blue eyes,   She is watch-ing and long-ing and wait-ing,   Where the
ev-er,   Till the sha-dows veil their skies,   But he loves to hold her lit-tle hands,   And

long white road-way lies.   And a song stirs in the si-lence, As the wind in the boughs a-
look in her sea-blue eyes,   And she sees the road by the pop-lars, Where they met in the by-gone

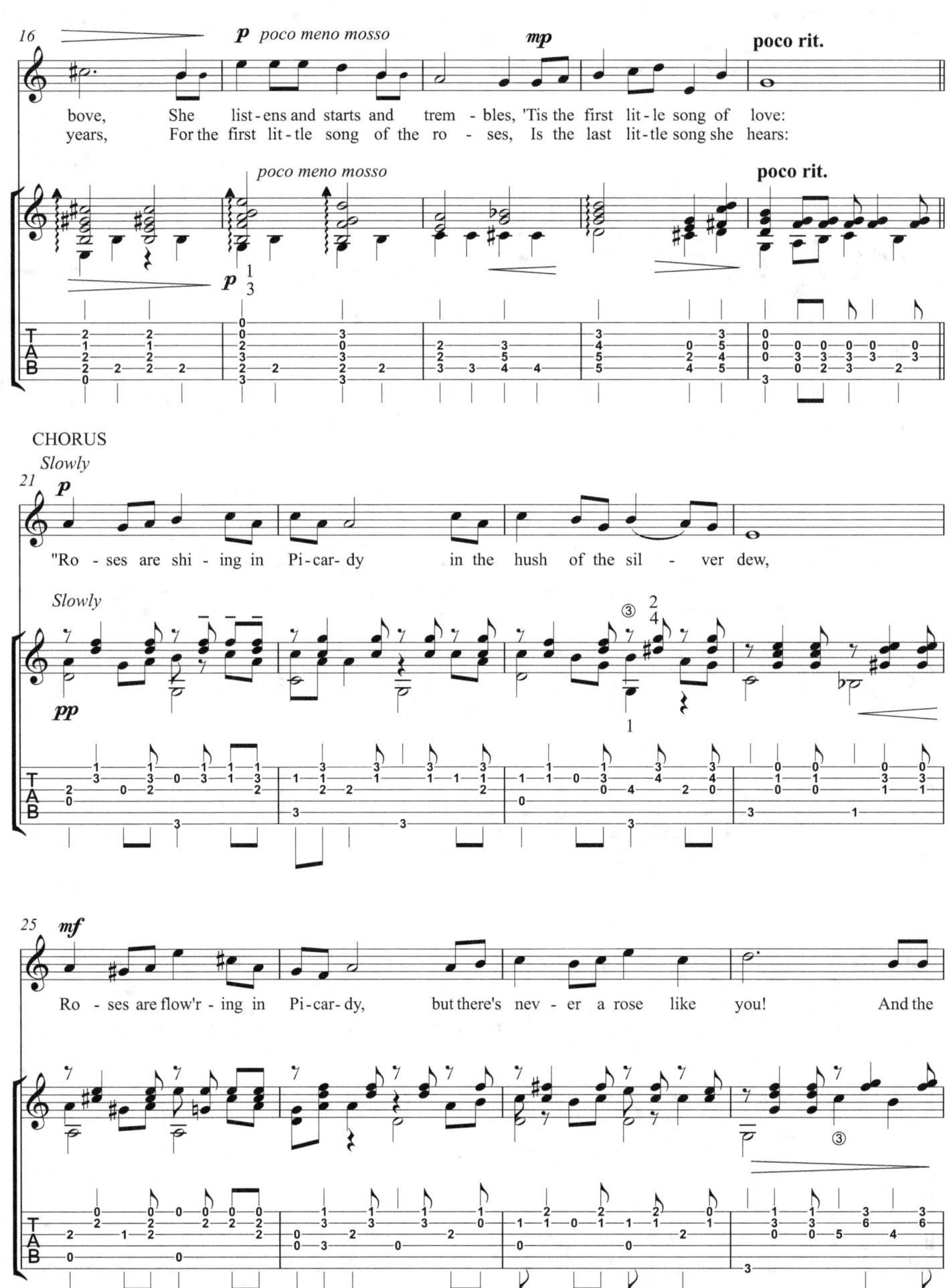

bove, She list-ens and starts and trem - bles, 'Tis the first lit-le song of love:
years, For the first lit-tle song of the ro - ses, Is the last lit-tle song she hears:

CHORUS

Slowly

"Ro - ses are shi - ing in Pi-car-dy in the hush of the sil - ver dew,

Ro - ses are flow'r - ing in Pi-car-dy, but there's nev - er a rose like you! And the

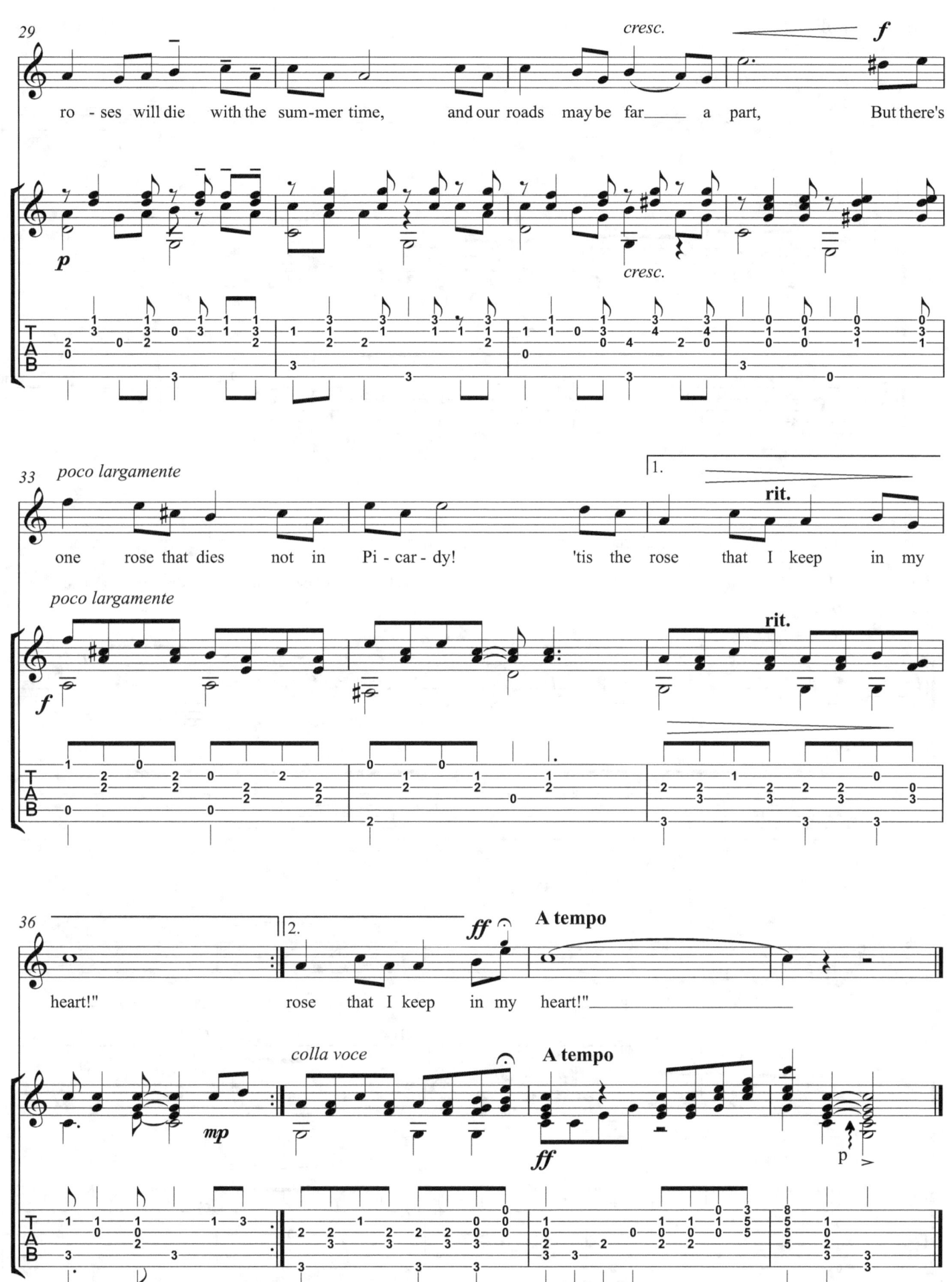

roses will die with the summer time, and our roads may be far___ apart, But there's

one rose that dies not in Pi-car-dy! 'tis the rose that I keep in my

heart!" rose that I keep in my heart!"___

Sylvia

Clinton Schollard

Oley Speaks

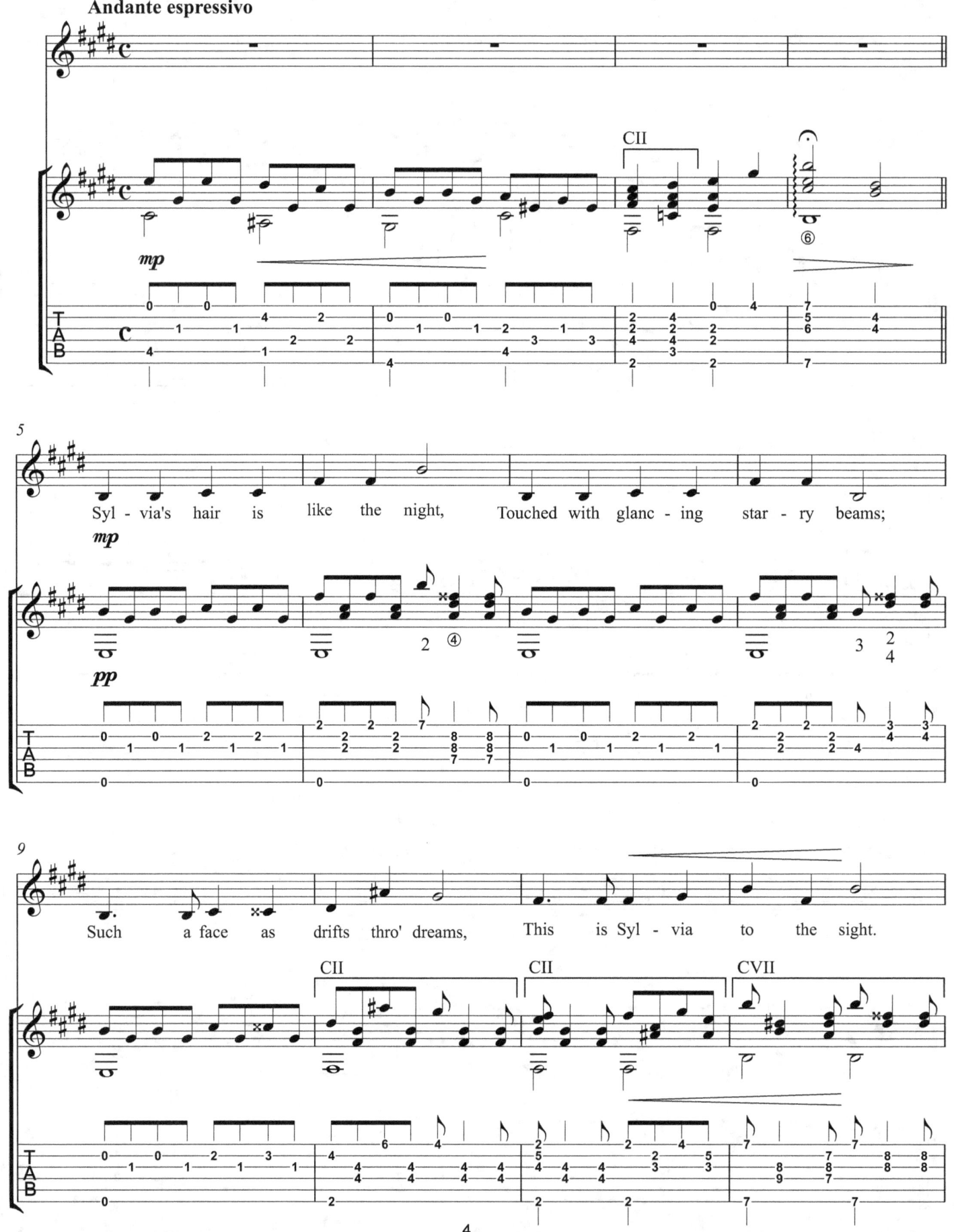

4

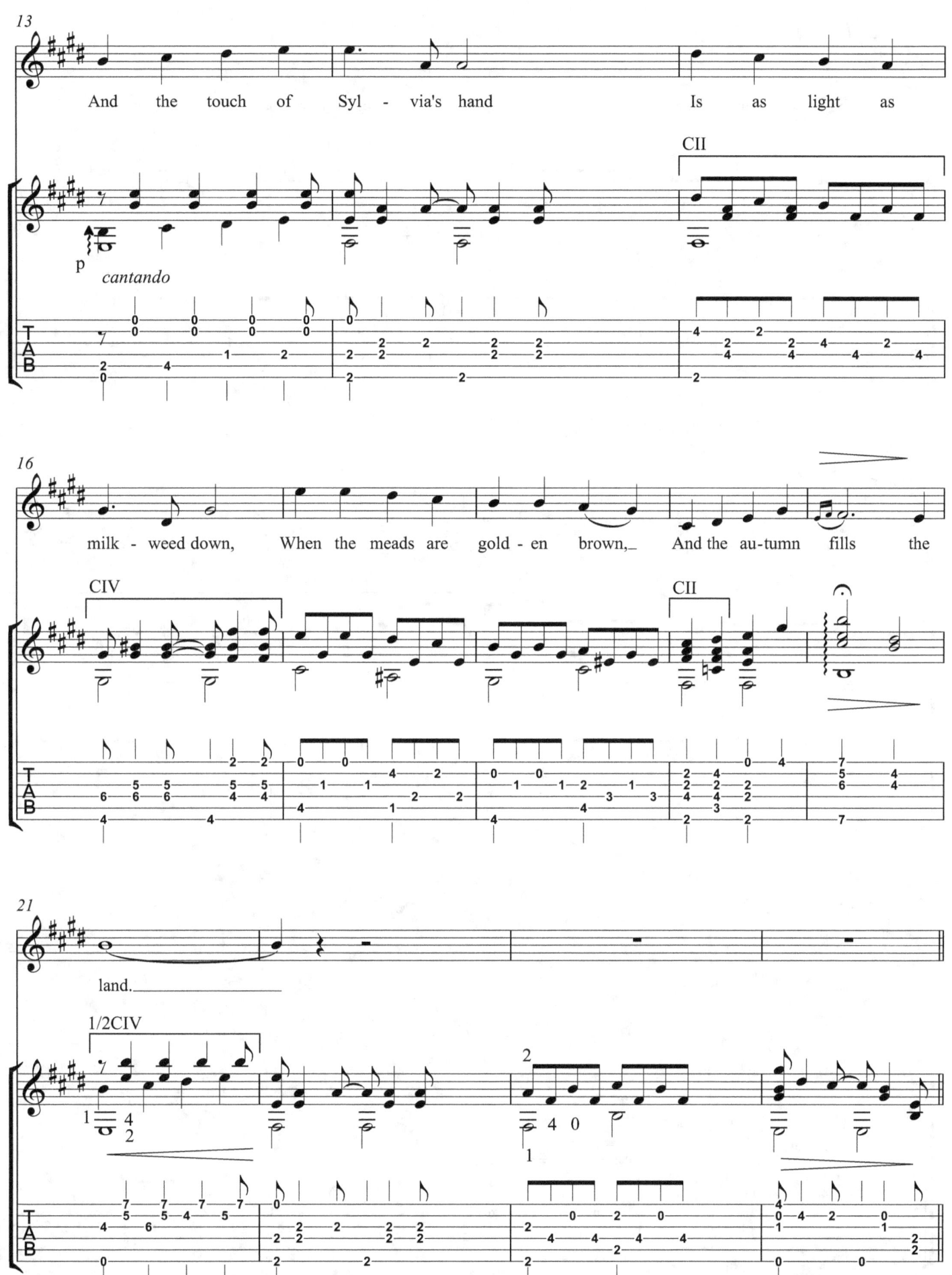

And the touch of Syl - via's hand   Is as light as milk - weed down,   When the meads are gold - en brown,_   And the au-tumn fills the land._

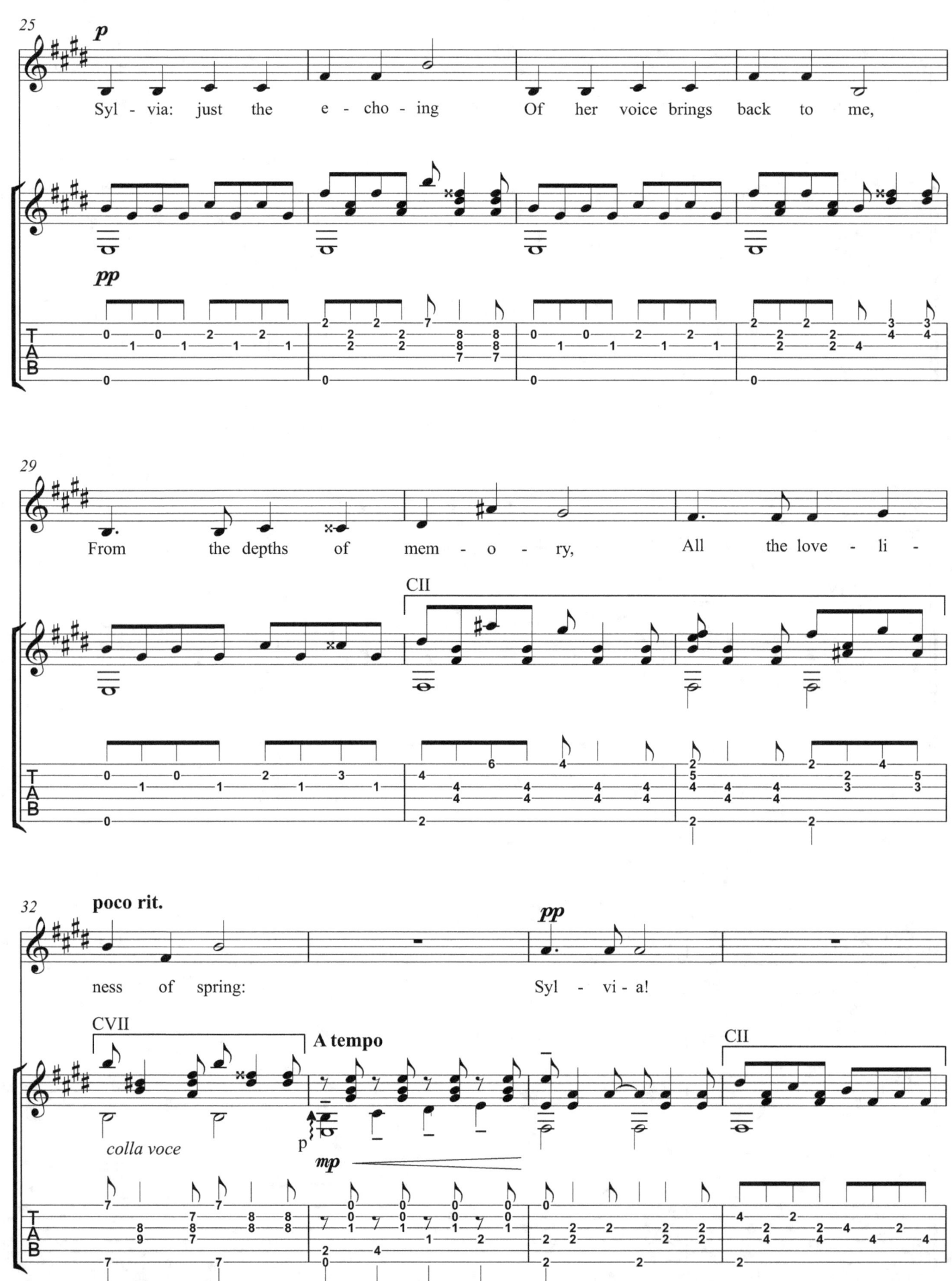

Syl - via: just the e - cho - ing Of her voice brings back to me,

From the depths of mem - o - ry, All the love - li-

poco rit.

ness of spring: Syl - vi - a!

A tempo

colla voce

6

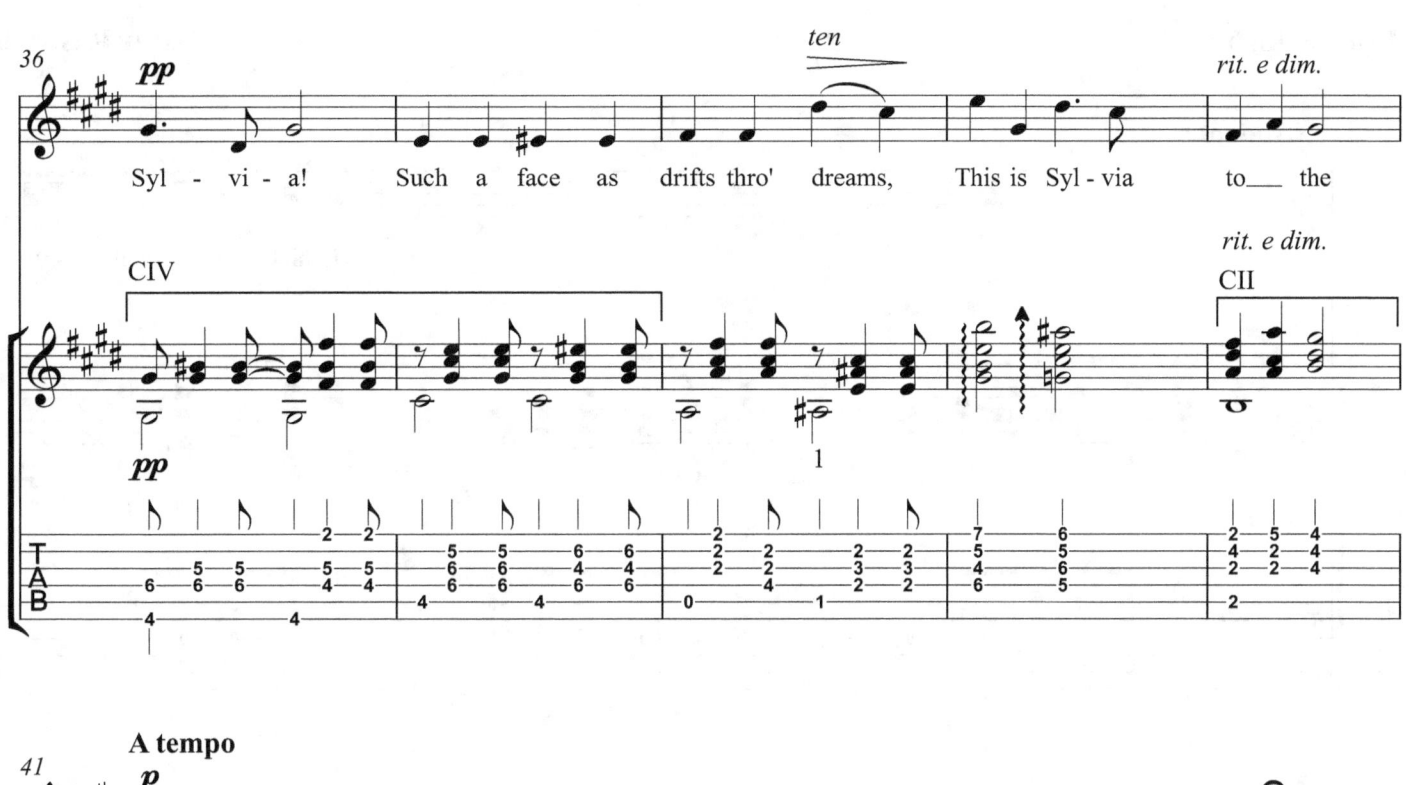

Syl - vi - a! Such a face as drifts thro' dreams, This is Syl - via to__ the

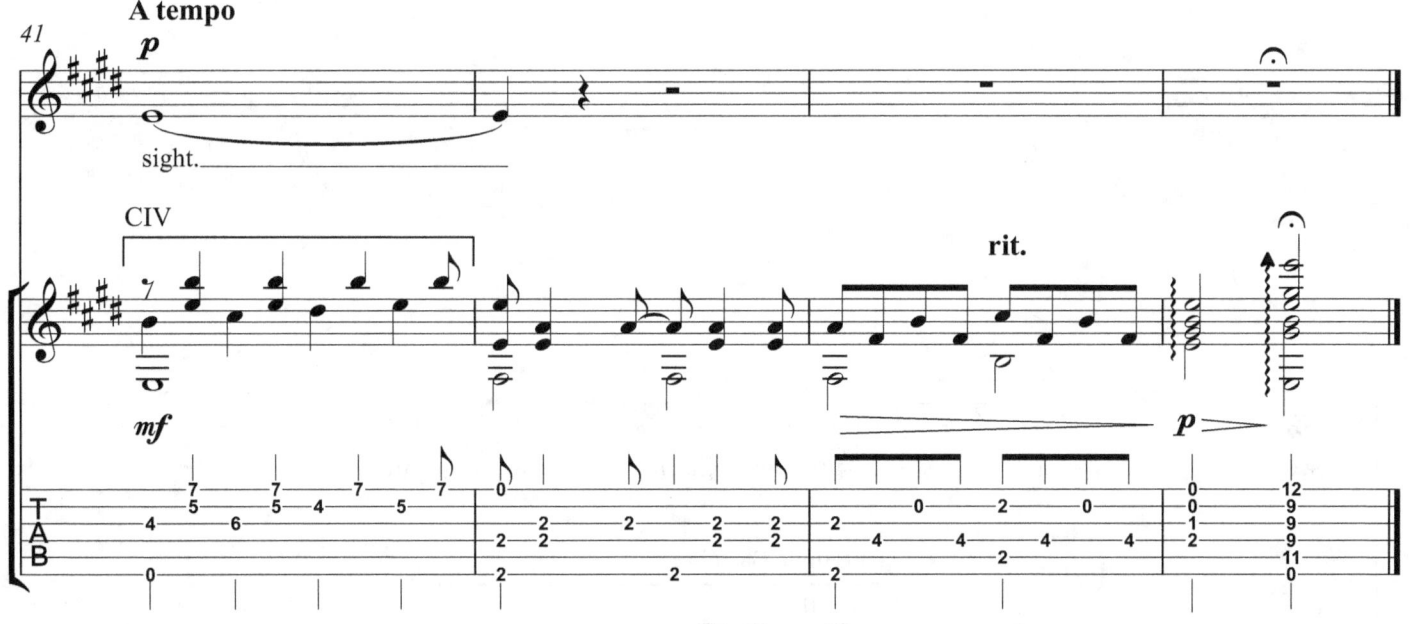

sight._____

Trees

Joyce Kilmer

Oscar Rasbach

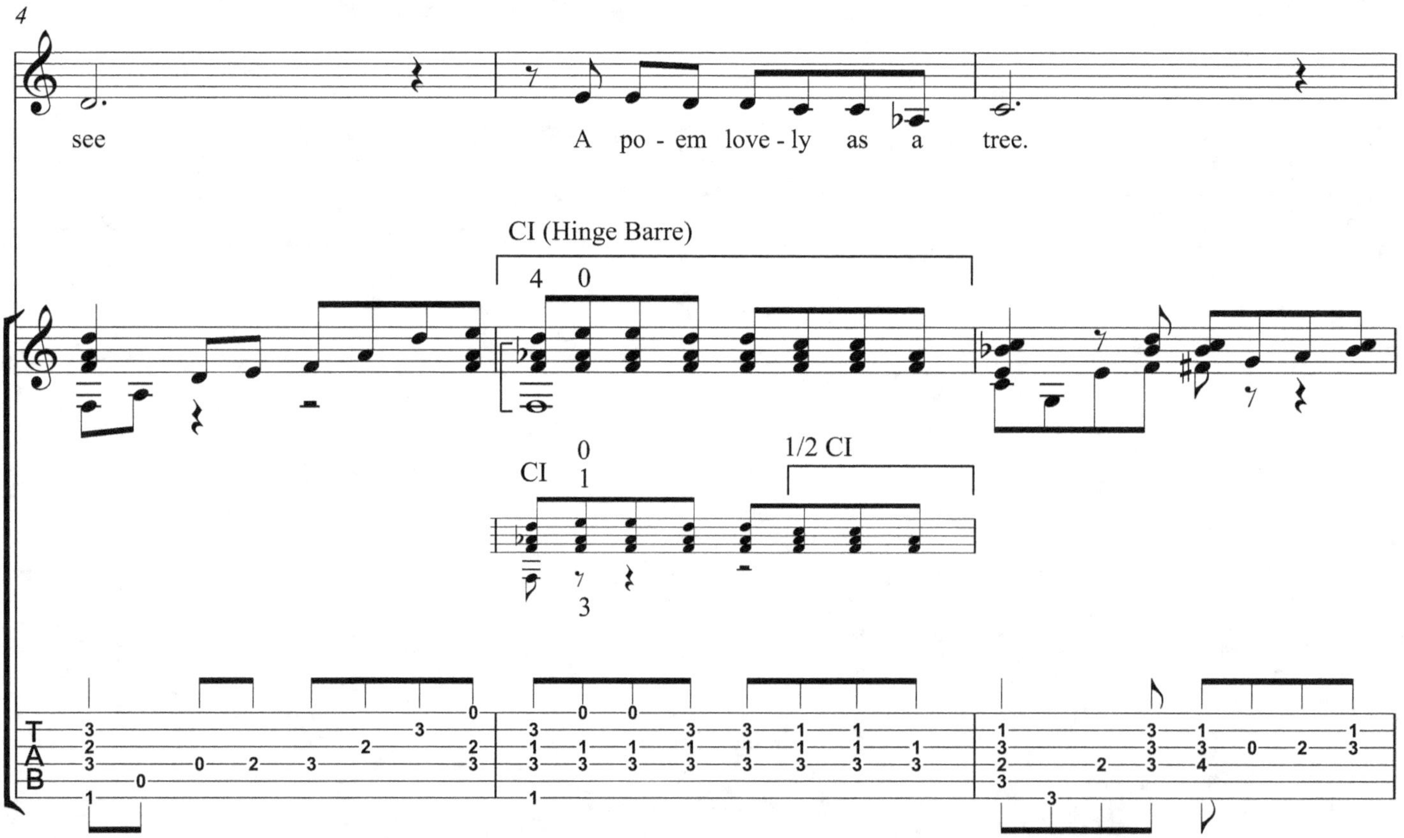

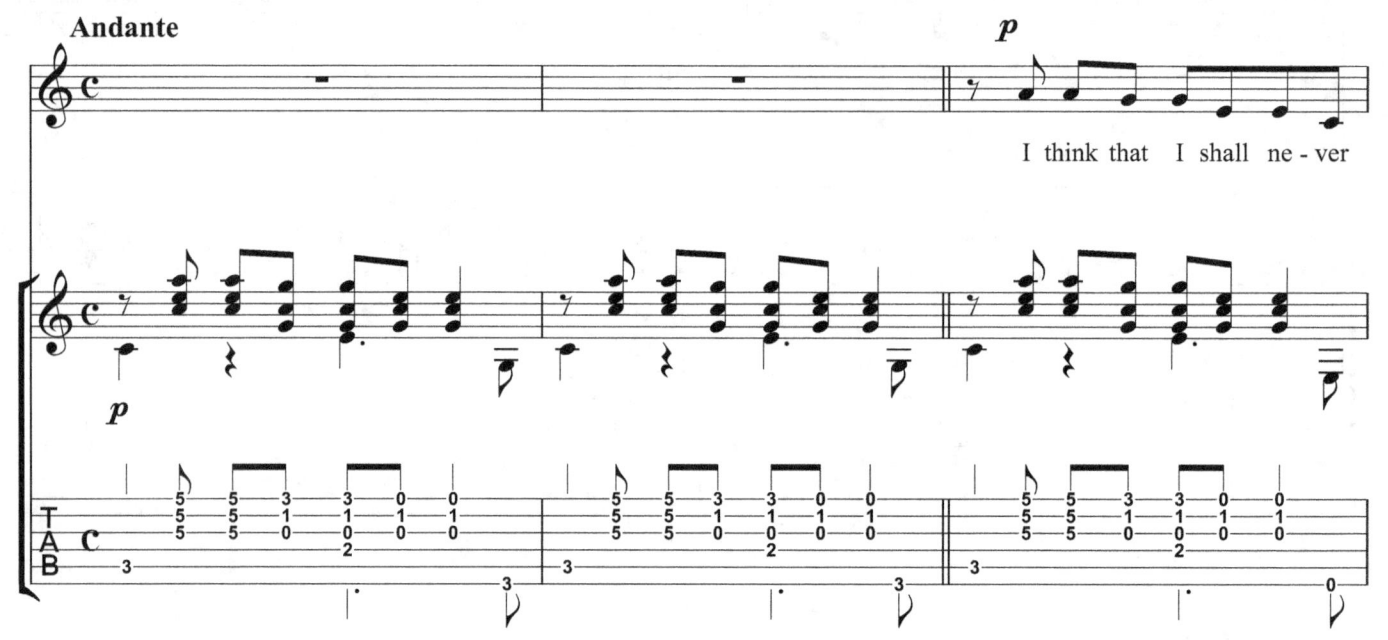

I think that I shall ne - ver

see

A po - em love - ly as a tree.

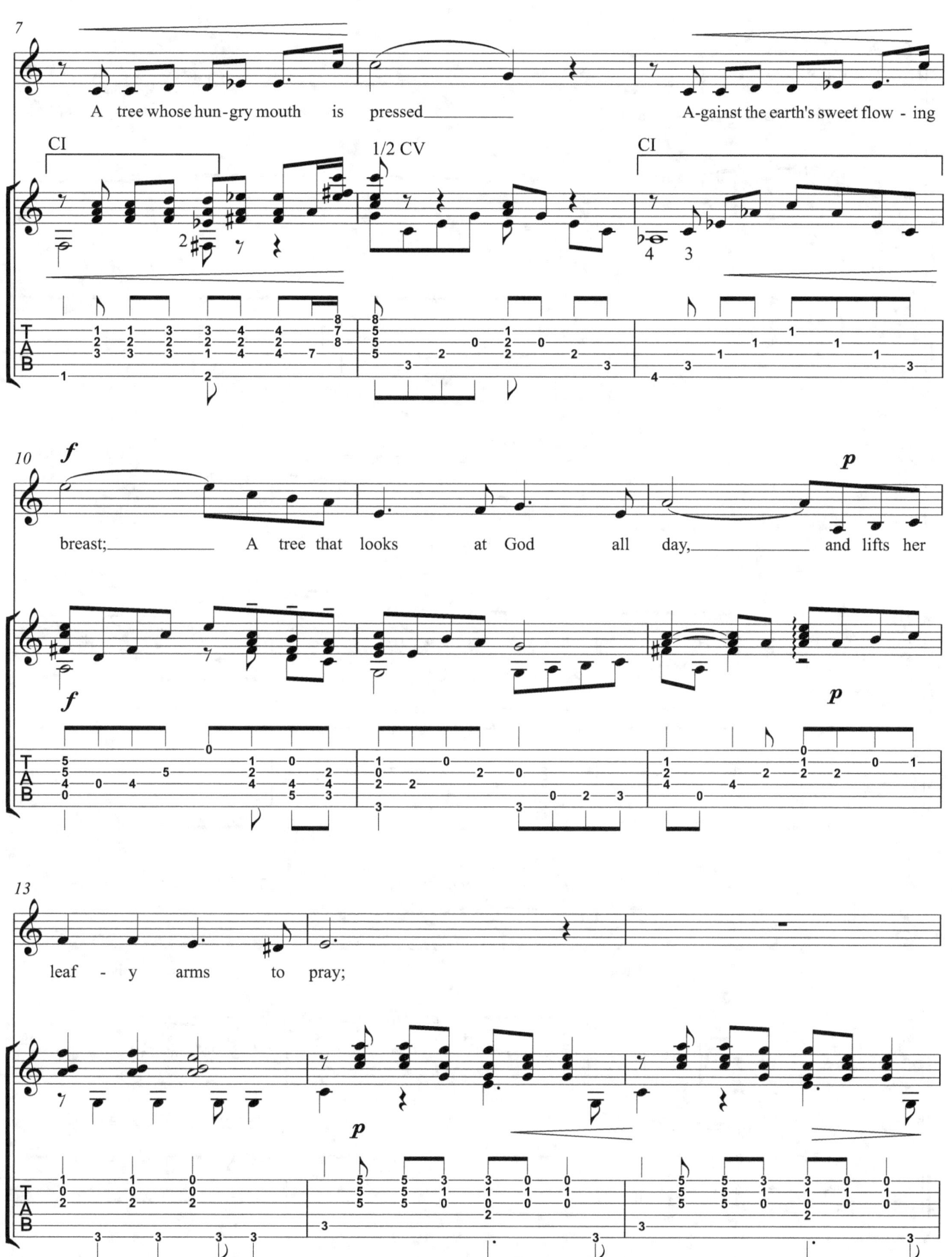

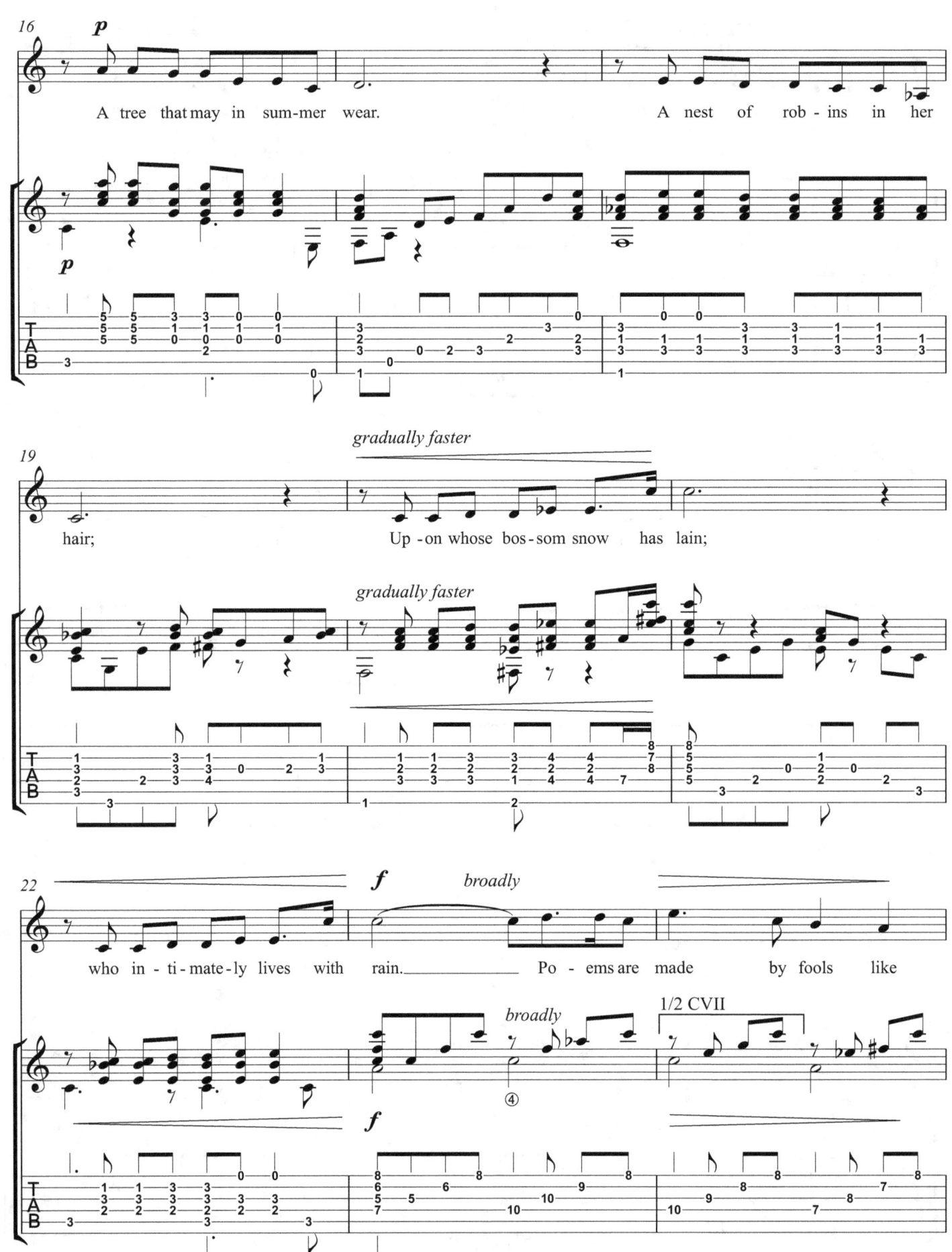

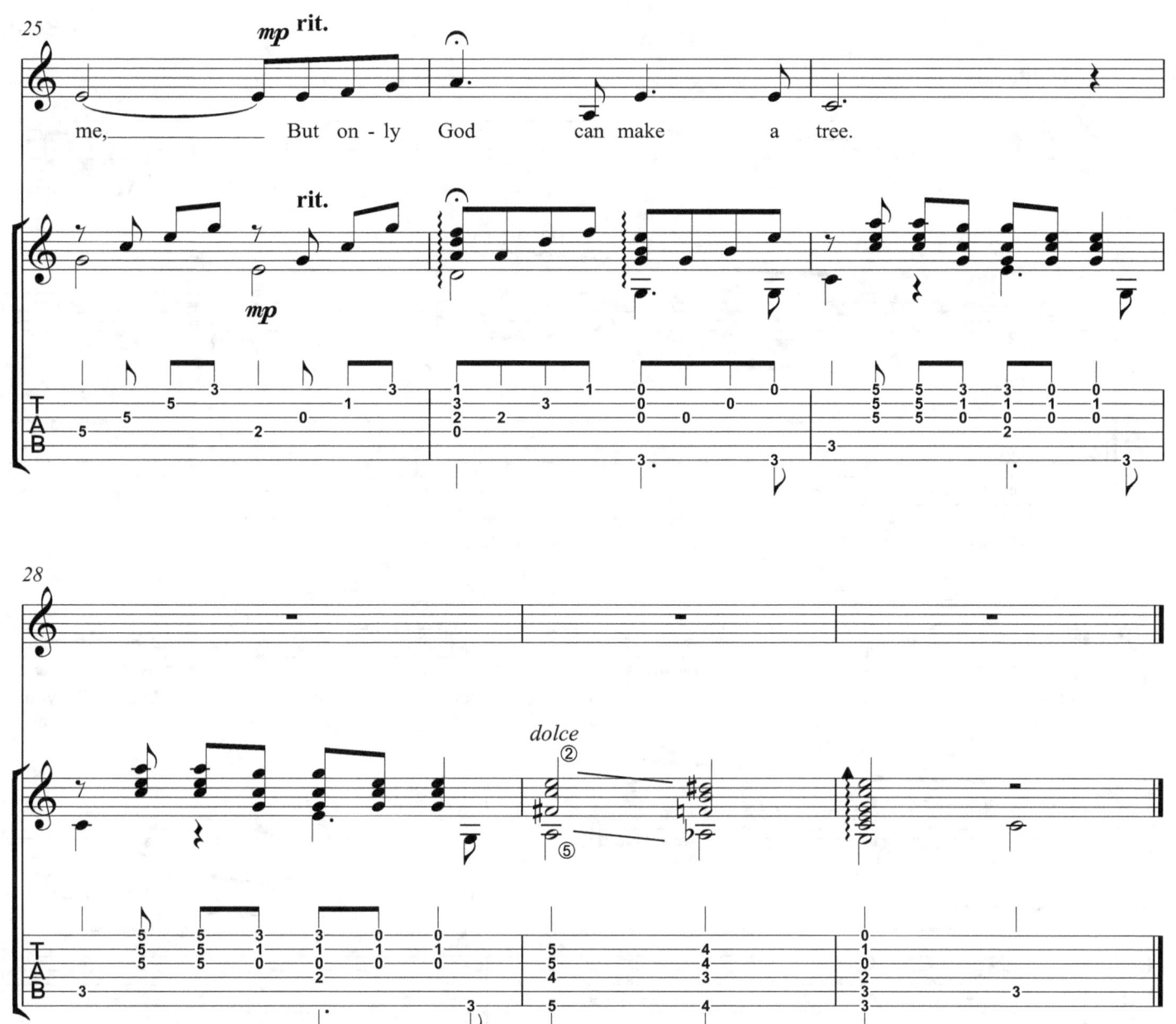

me,_____ But on - ly God   can make   a   tree.

A Perfect Day

Carrie Jacobs-Bond

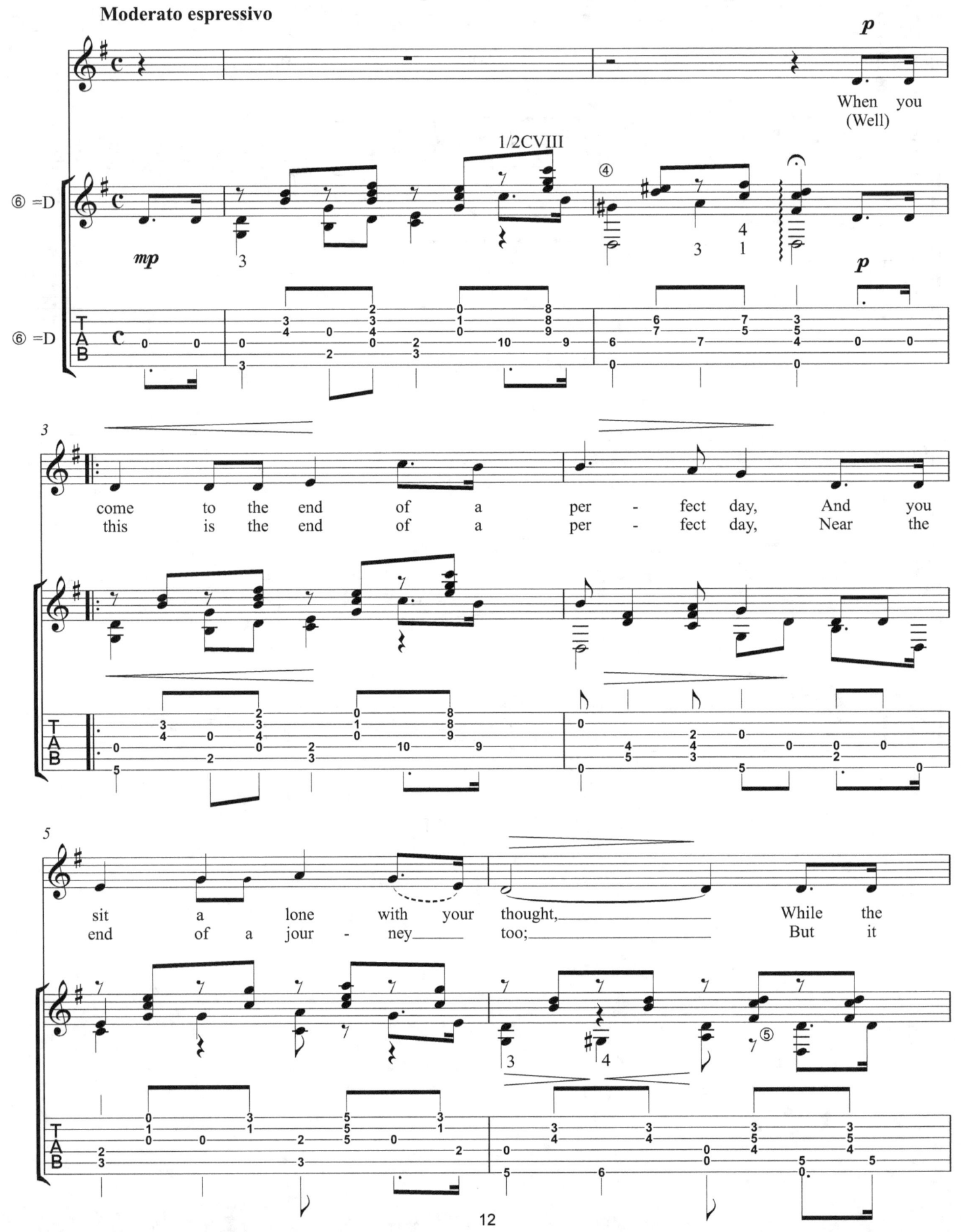

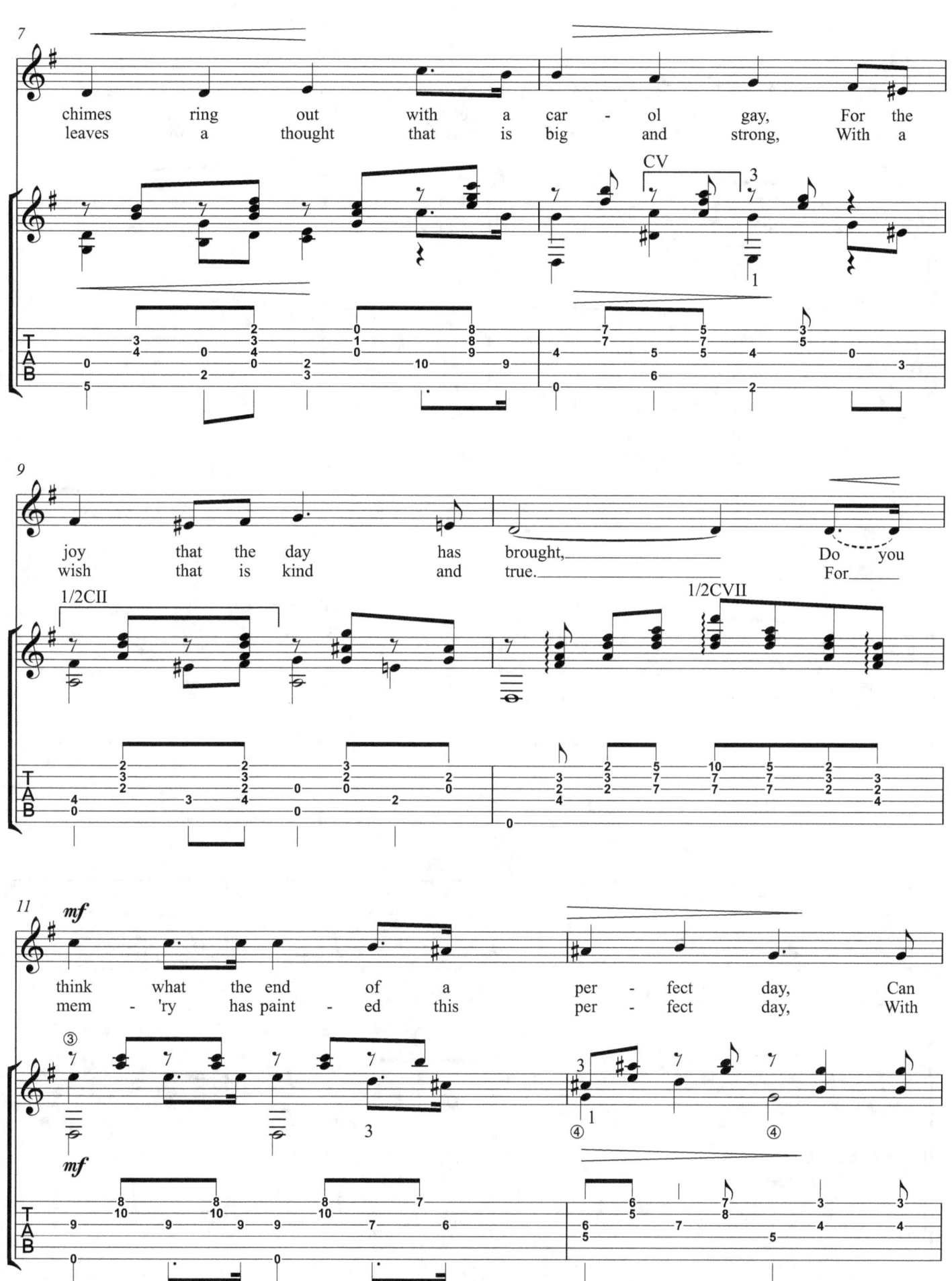

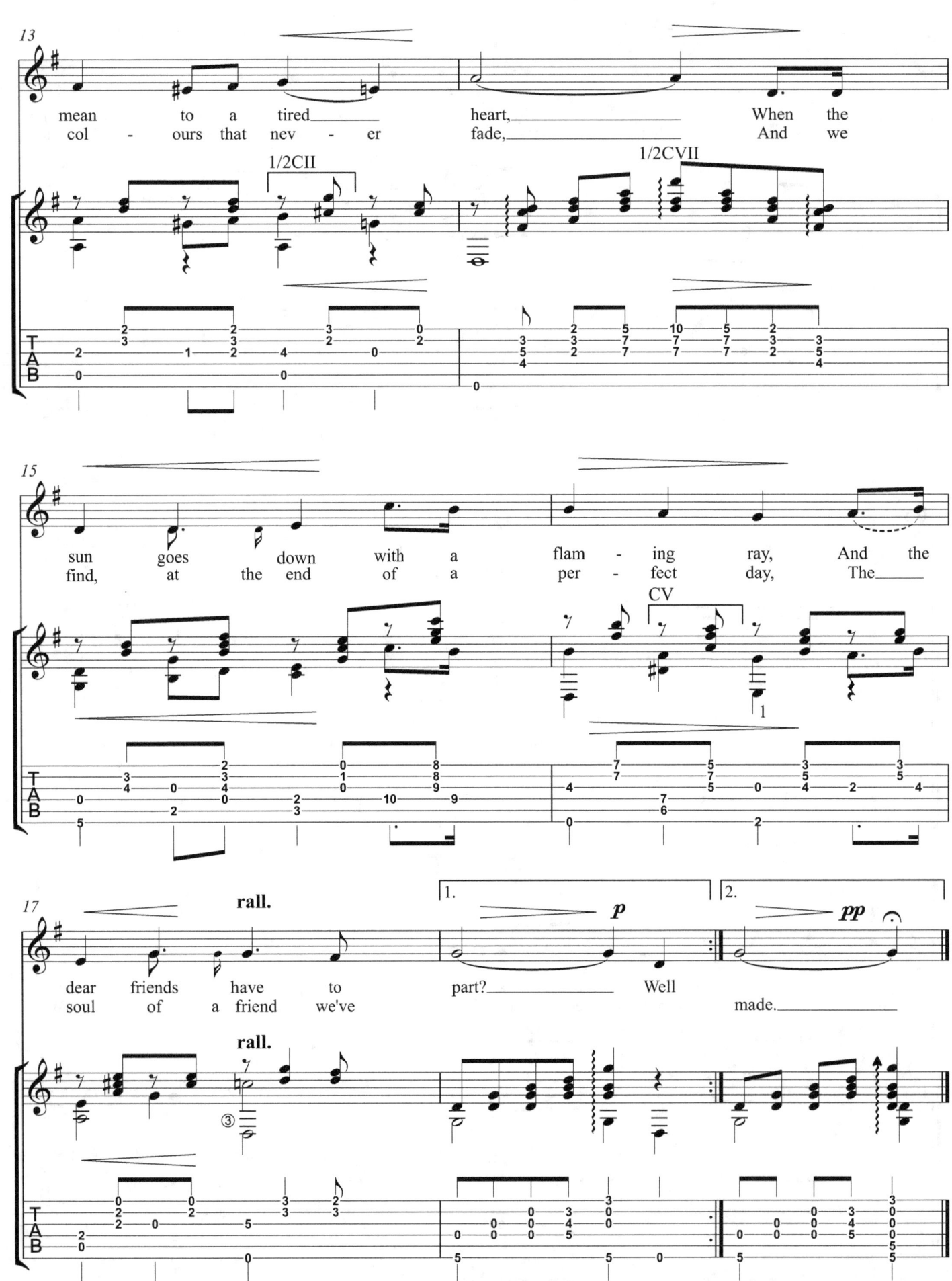

At Dawning (I Love You)

Nelle Richmond Eberhart

Charles Wakefileld Cadman

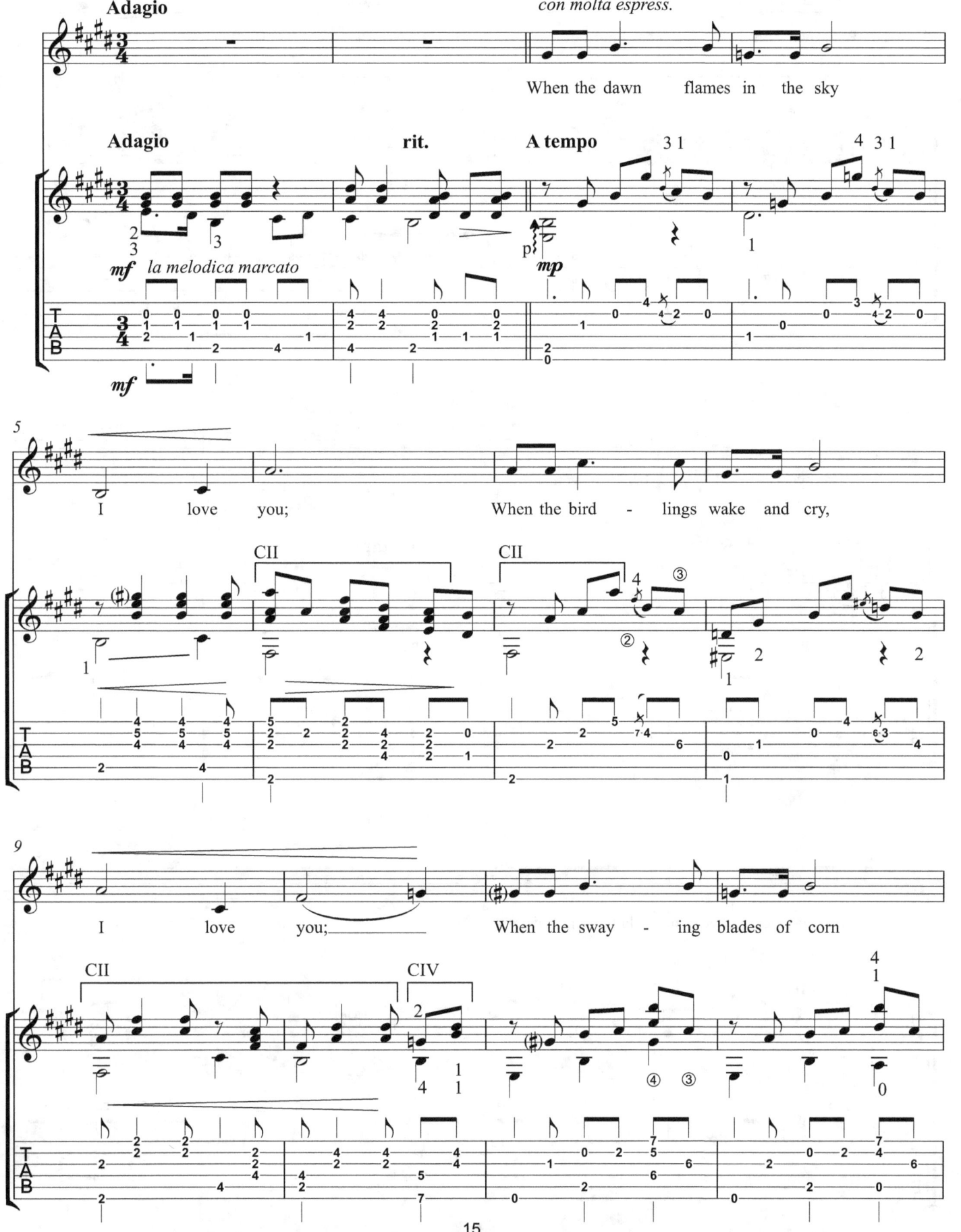

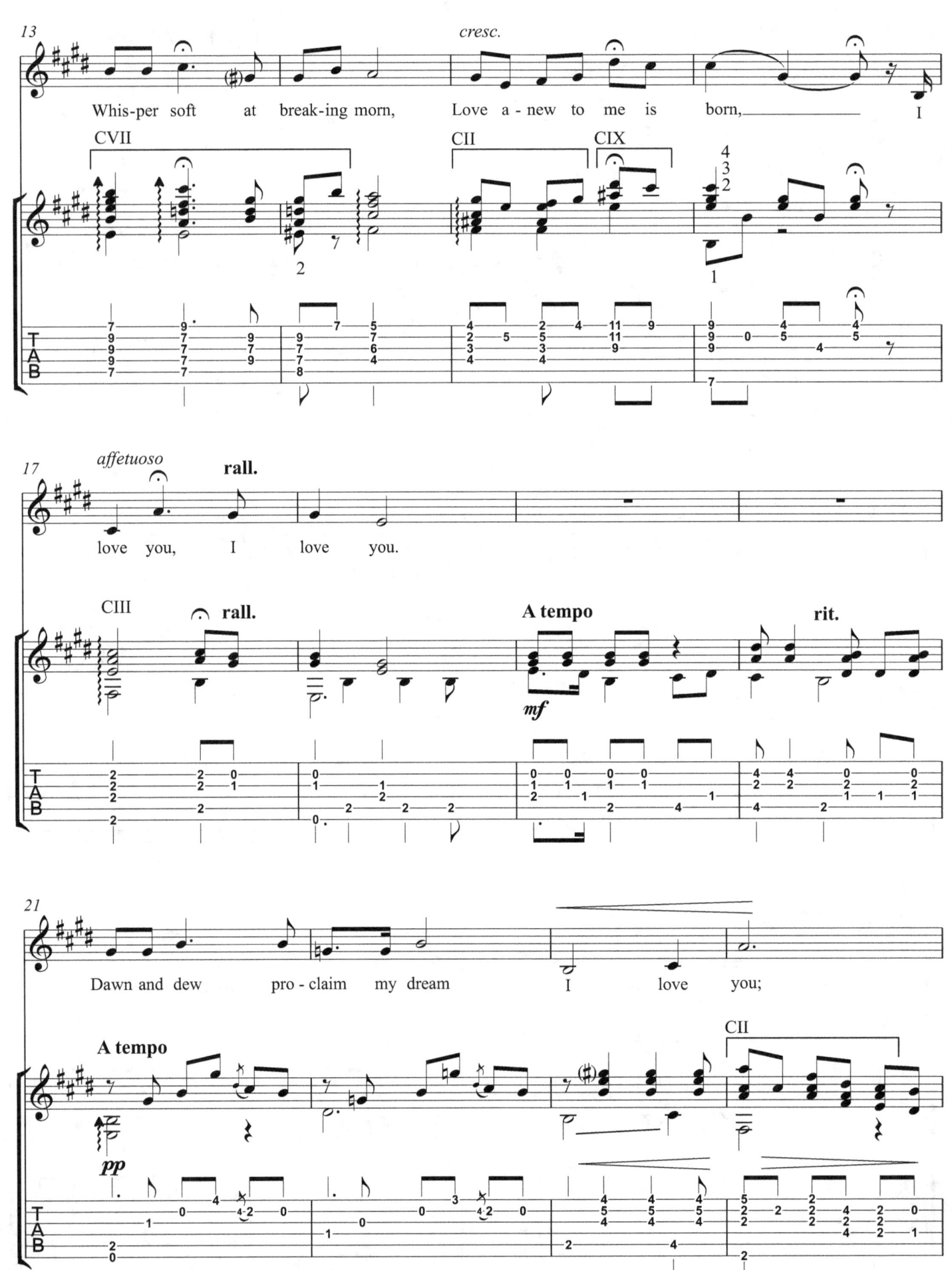

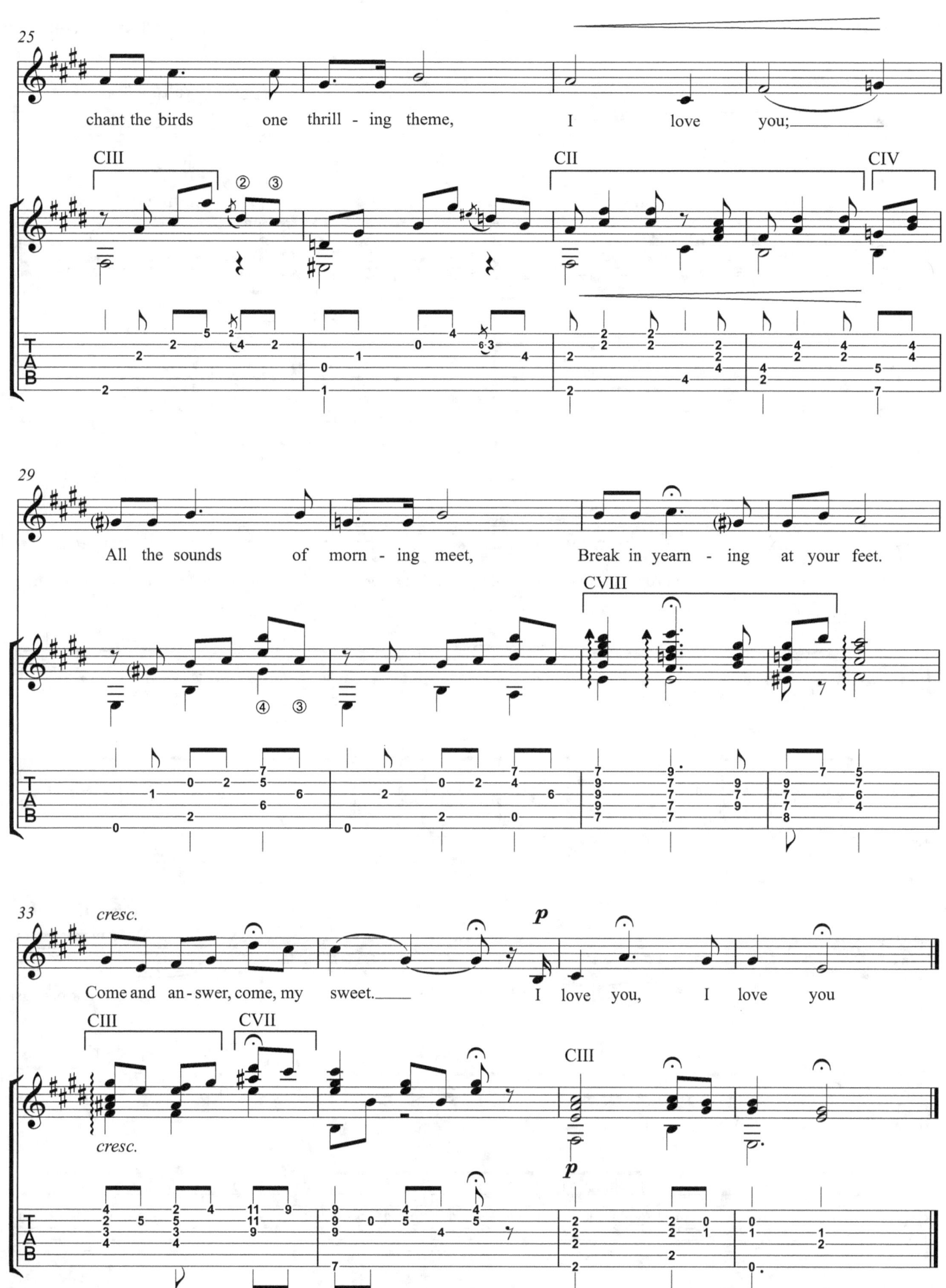

chant the birds   one thrill - ing theme,   I   love   you;____

All the sounds   of morn - ing meet,   Break in yearn - ing   at your feet.

Come and an - swer, come, my   sweet.____   I love you,   I love   you

I Hear You Calling Me

Harold Harford   Charles Marshall

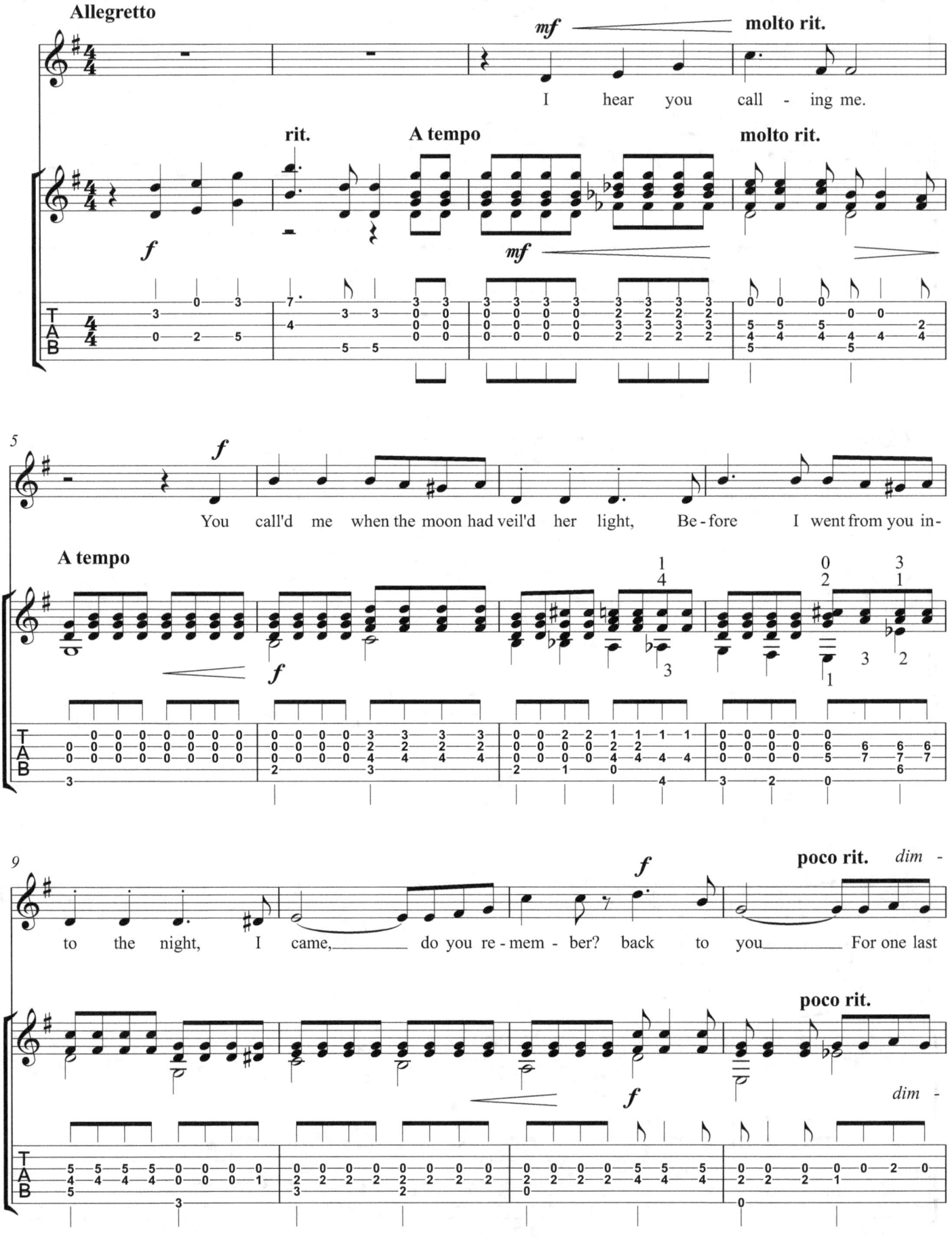

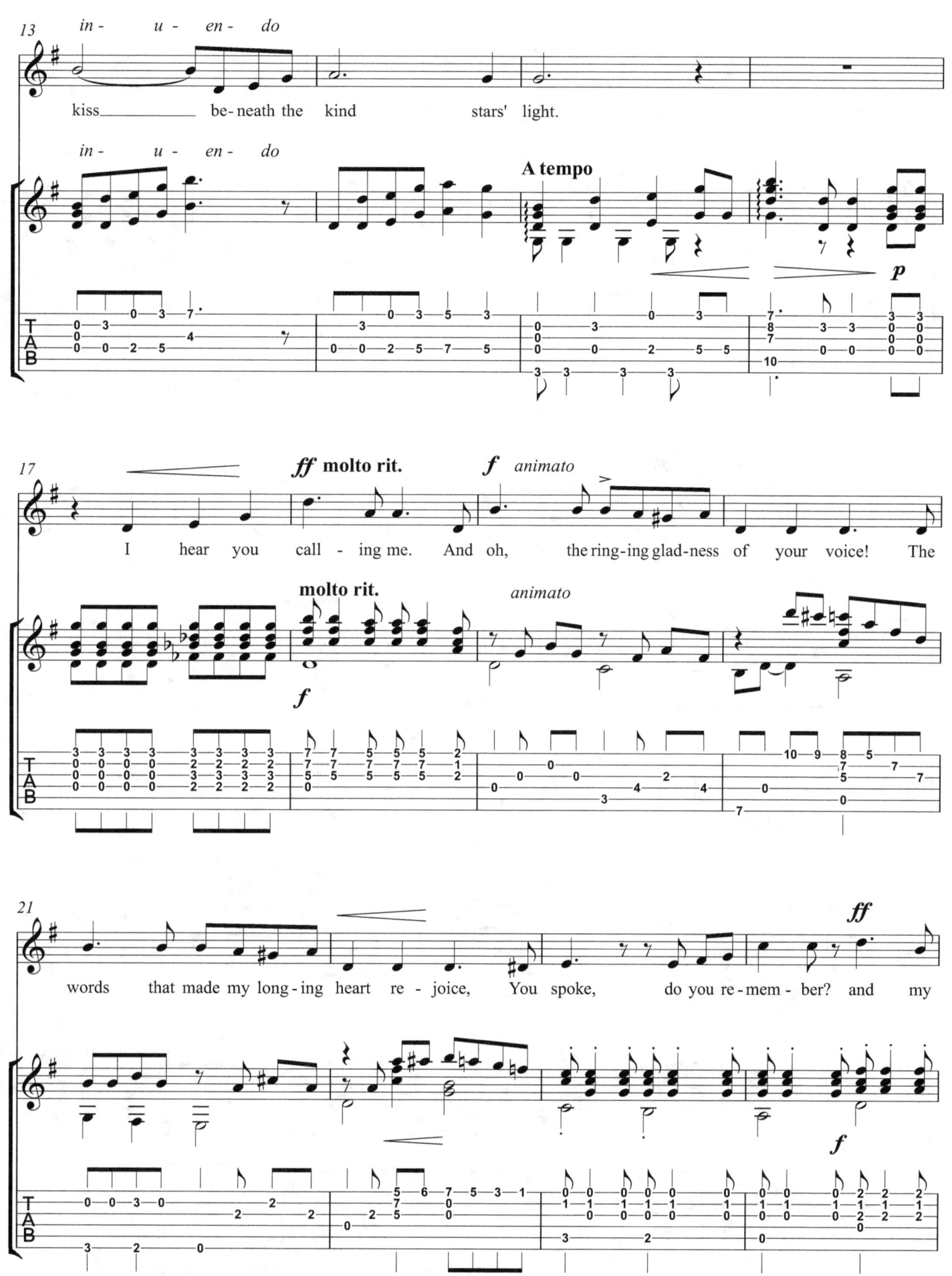

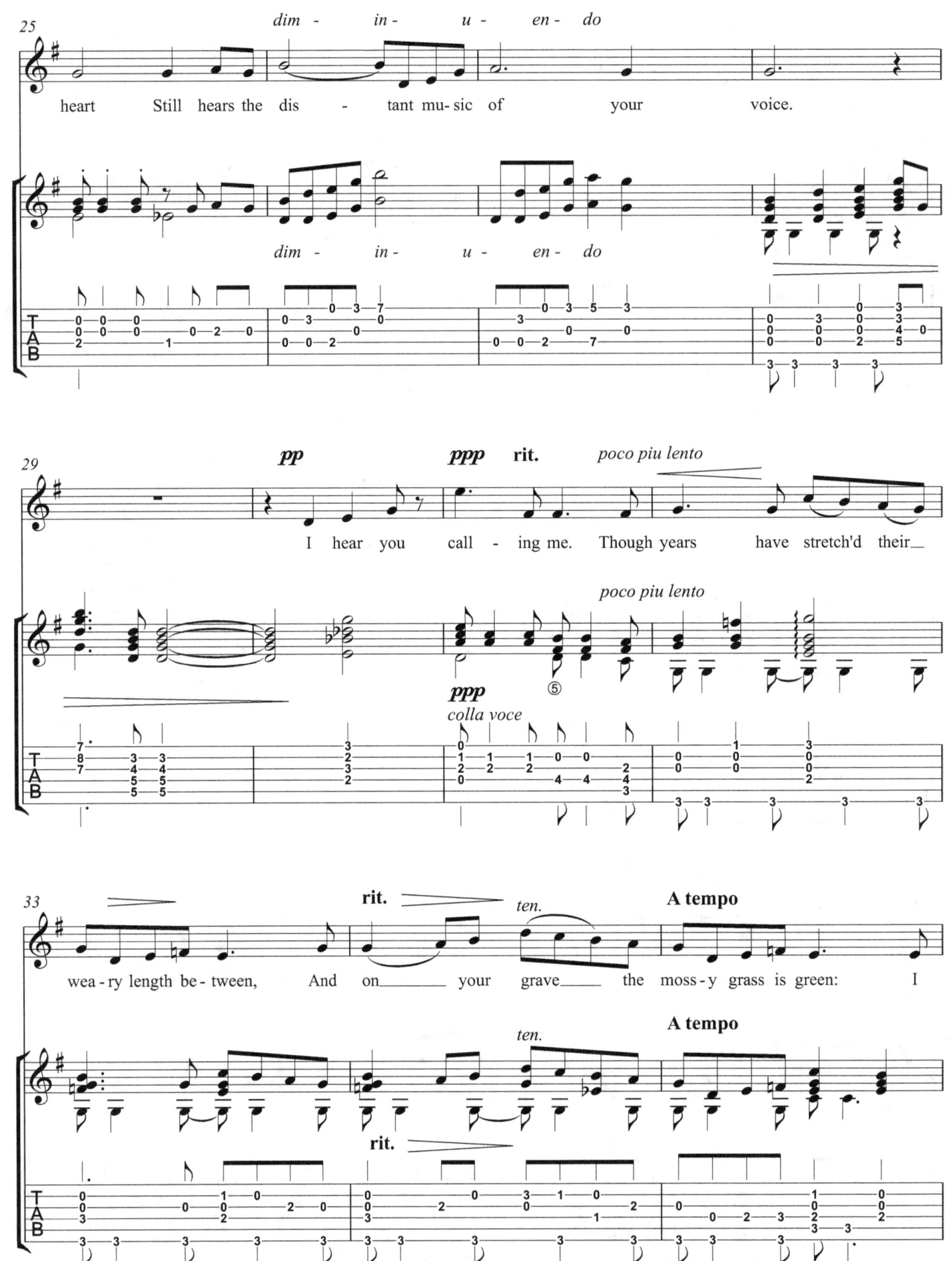

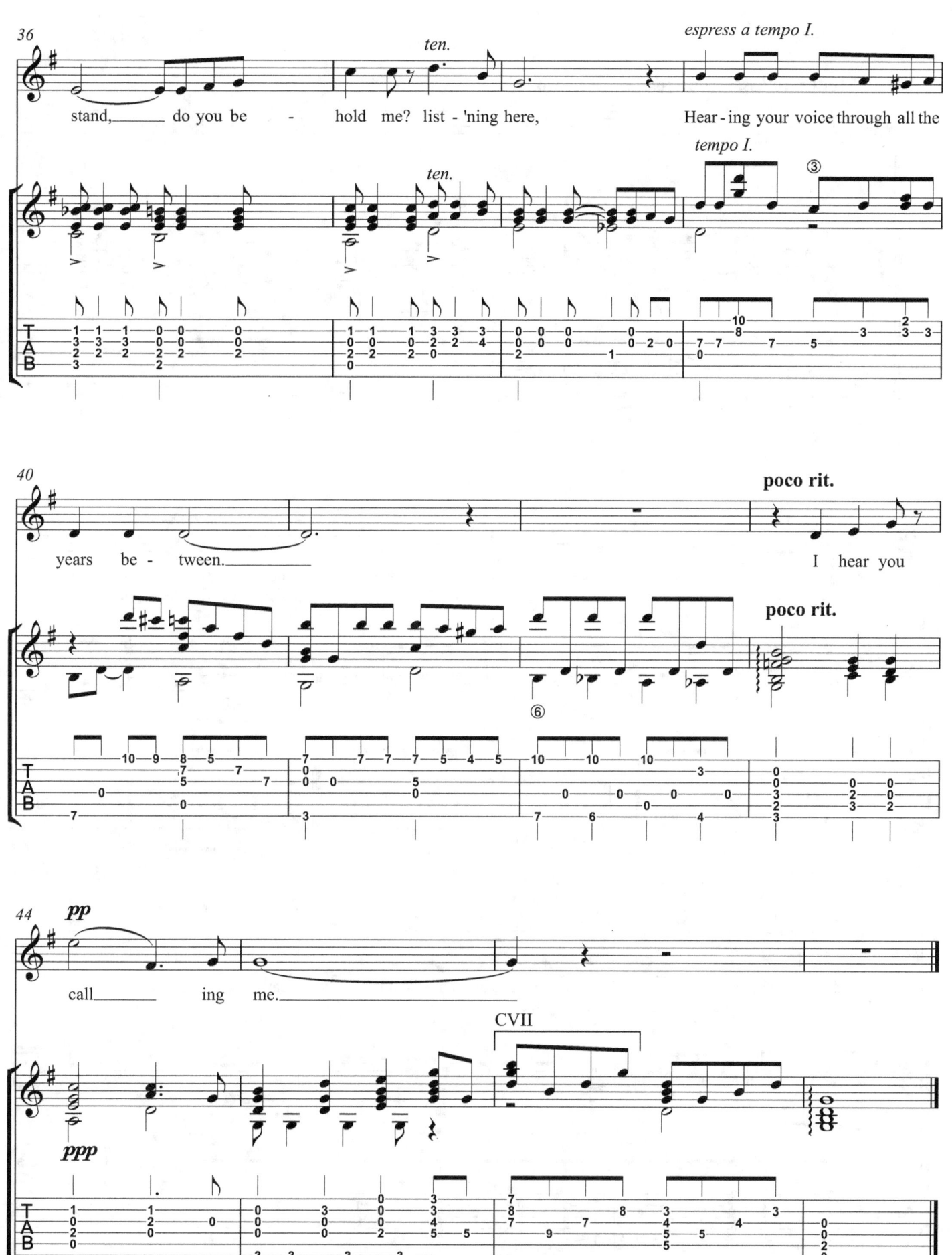

Kashmiri Song (Pale Hands I Loved)

Lawrence Hope

Amy Woodforde Finden

Moderato assai, con molto sentimento

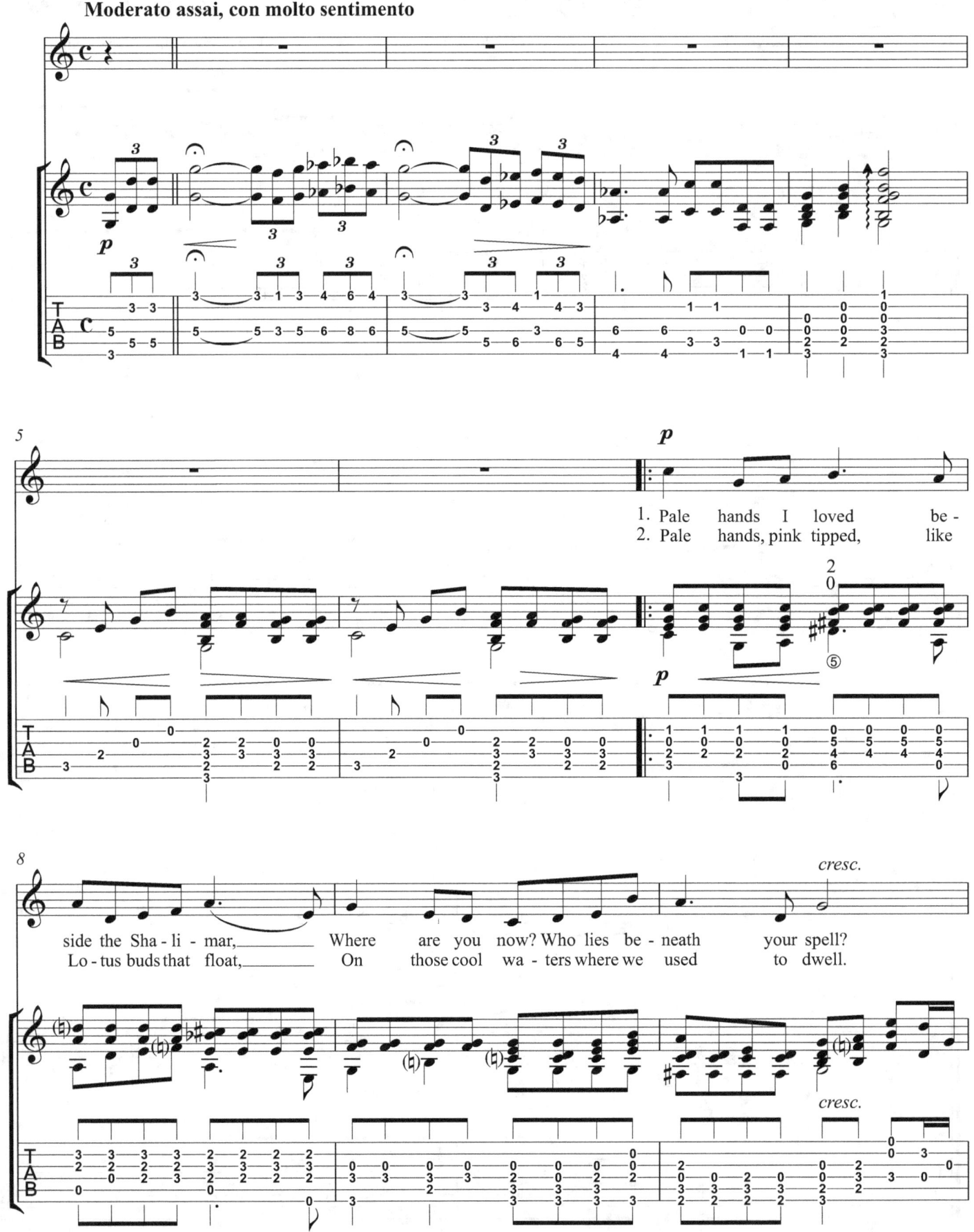

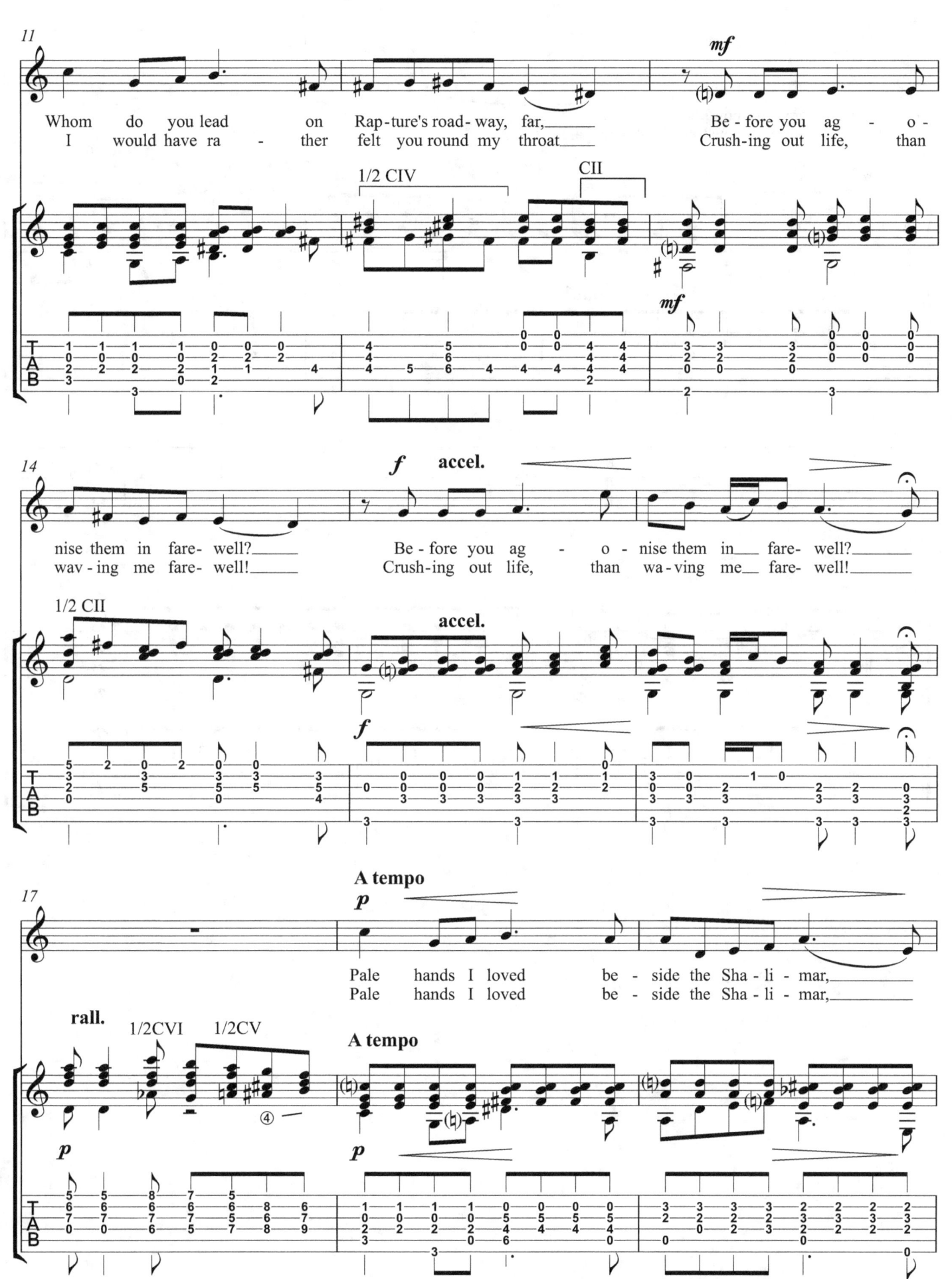

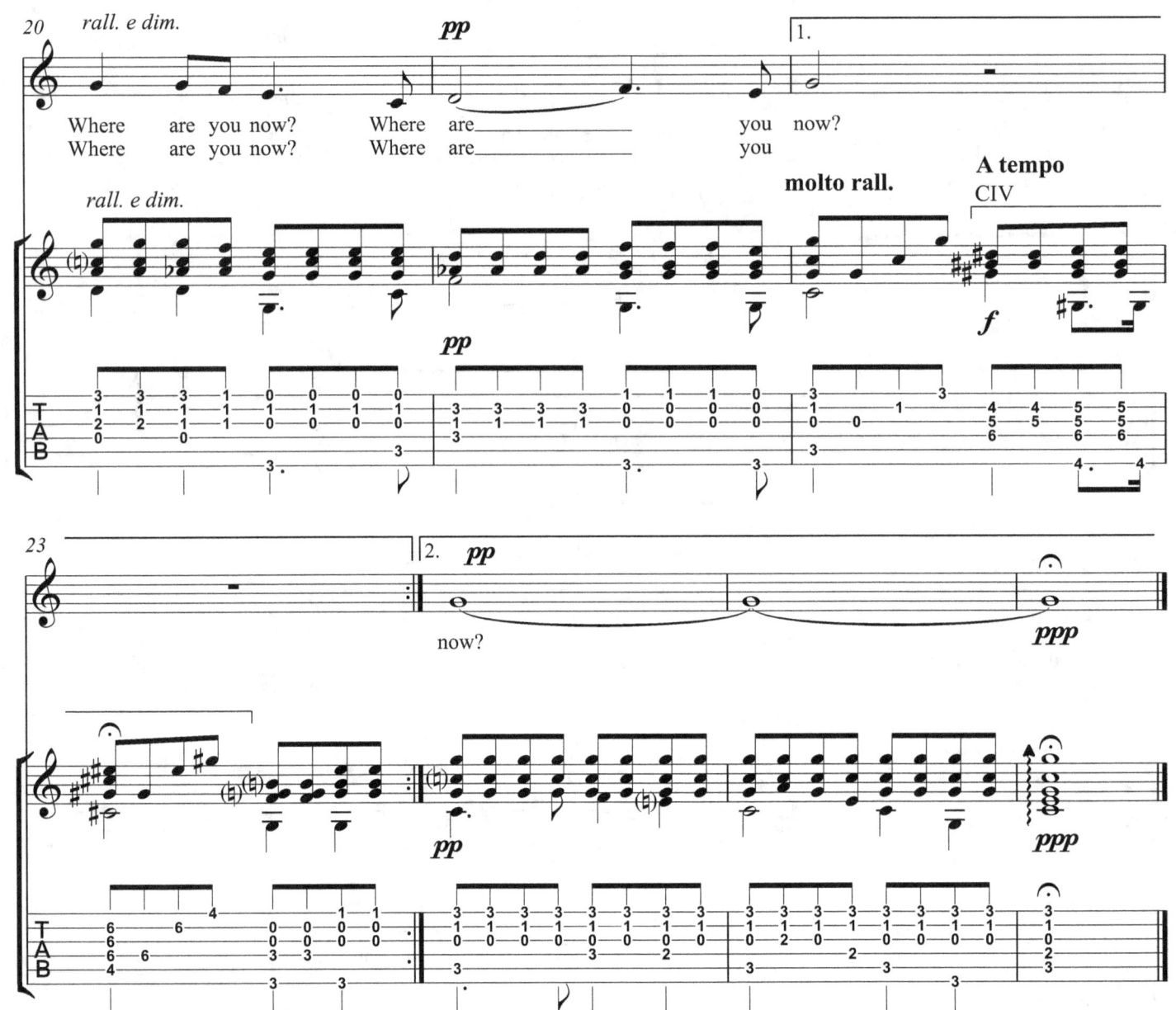

Where are you now? Where are _____ you now?
Where are you now? Where are _____ you

now?

UNTIL

Nº 1 in D♭   Nº 2 in E♭   Nº 3 in F   Nº 4 in G

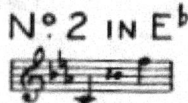 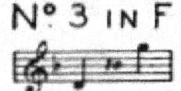 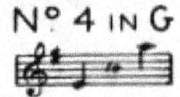

SONG

THE WORDS BY

EDWARD TESCHEMACHER

THE MUSIC BY

WILFRID SANDERSON.

75 CENTS

BOOSEY & HAWKES

Until

E.Teschemacher

Wilfed Sanderson

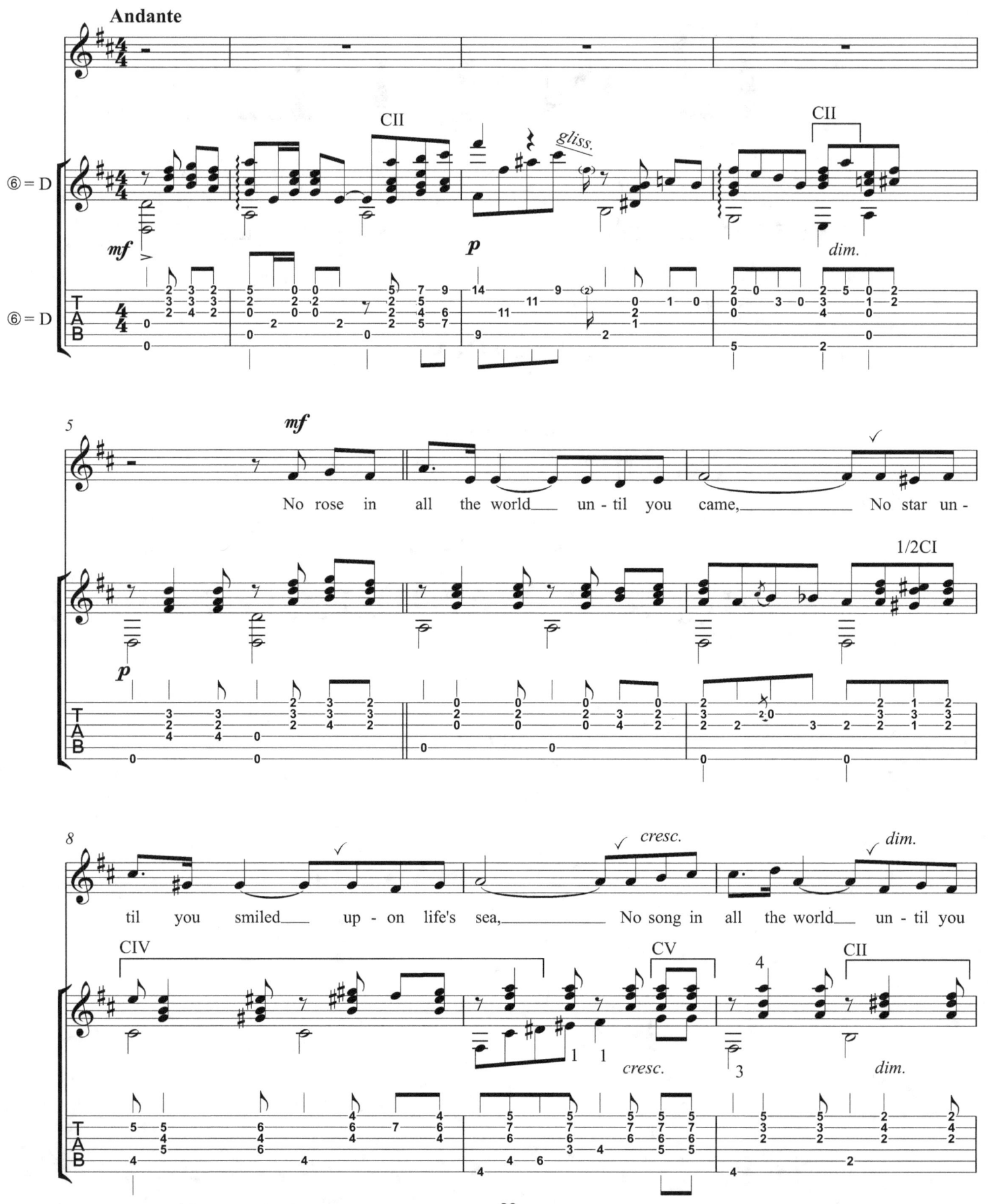

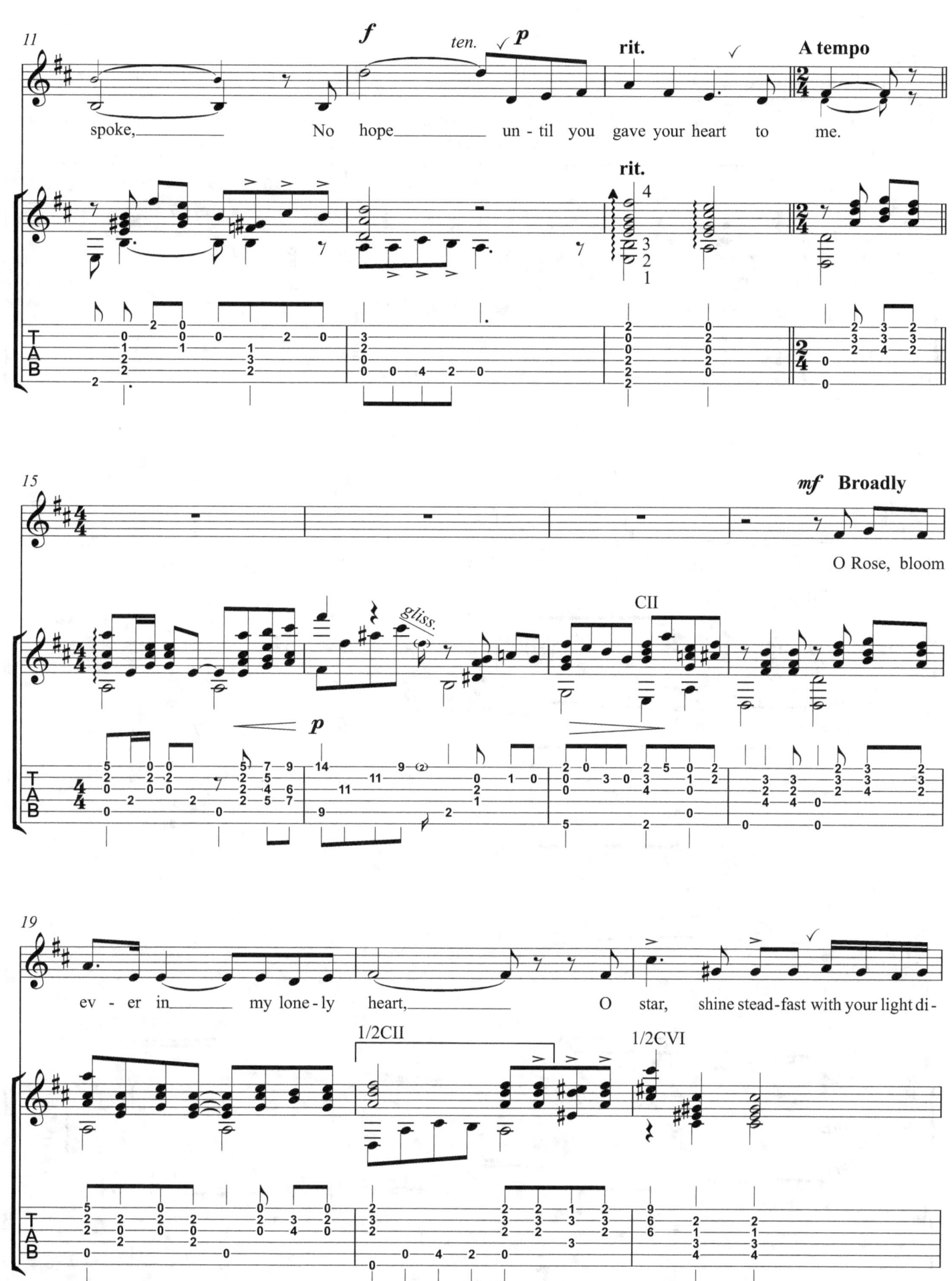

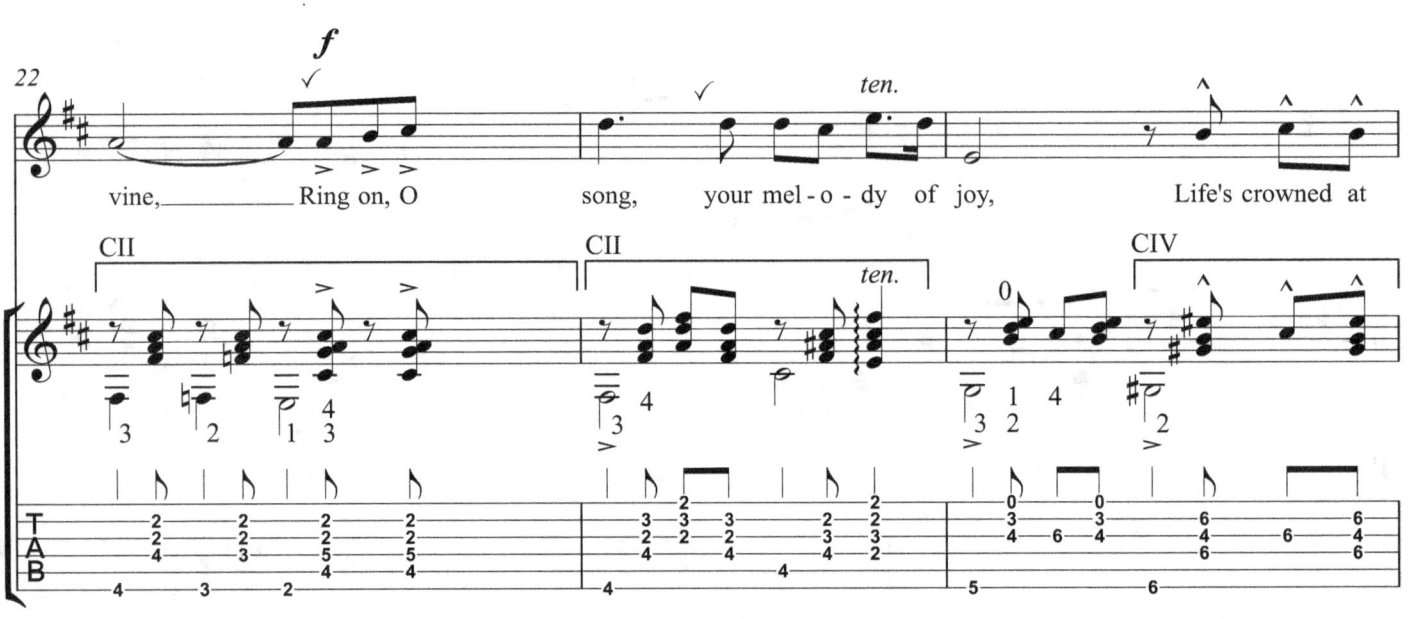

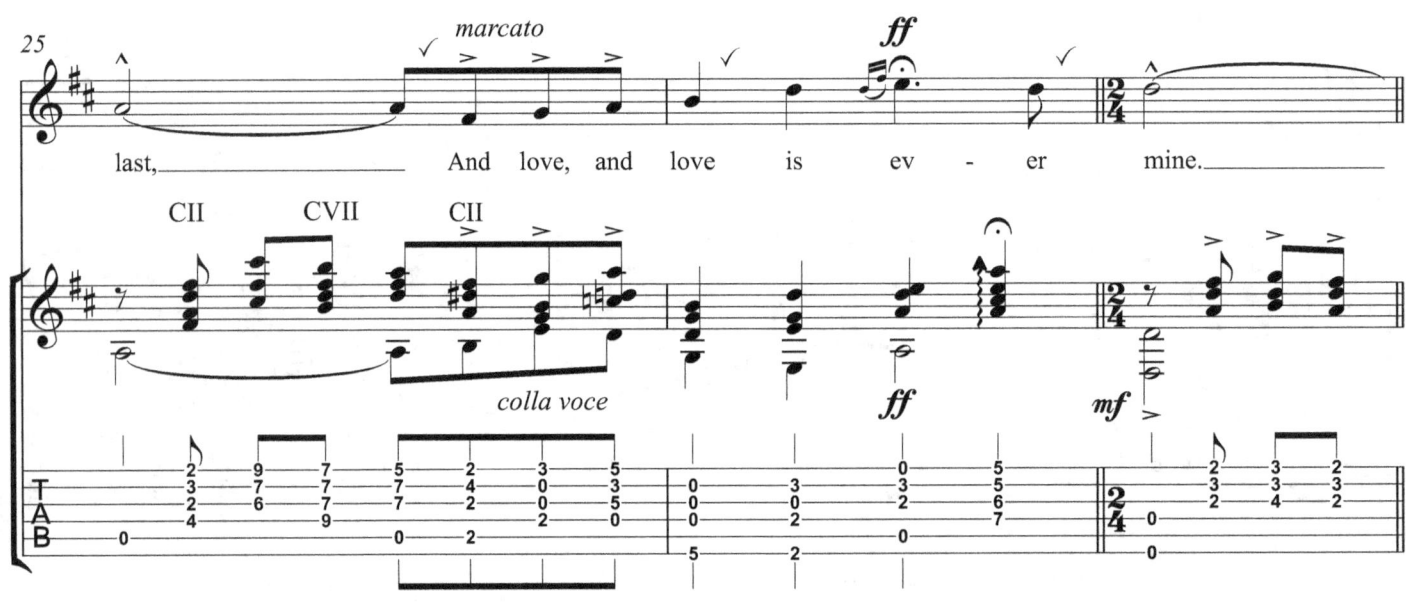

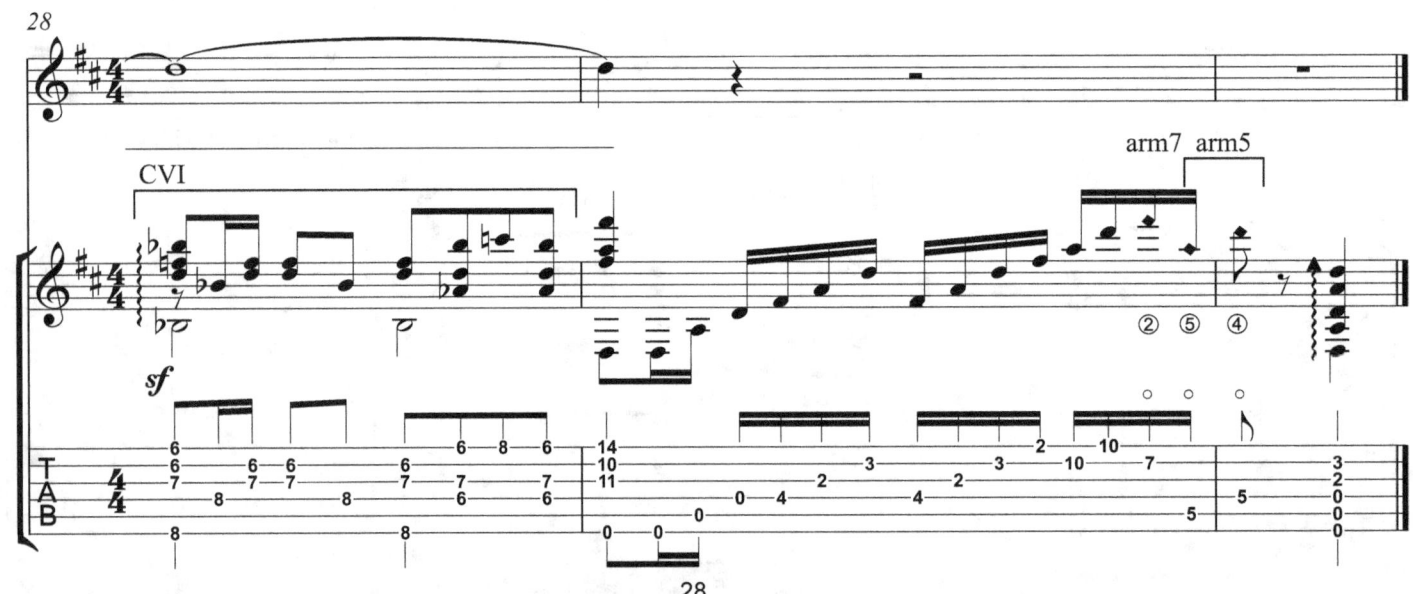

Available to purchase at lulu.com

Guitar Publications

Guitar Folksong Duets Volume 1:

A collection of pieces for pupils and teacher to play together: Danny Boy, Down by the Sally Gardens, My Love is like a Red Rose, and many more

Guitar Folksong Duets Volume 3

A third collection of duets for pupil and teacher. Included in this volume: Blow Away The Morning Dew; Blow The Wind Southerly; Carol; Go To Sleep; Grass Is Green, and many more

The Robert Burns Songbook for Guitar and Voice Vol 1

A collection of nineteen of Burns' songs for guitar and voice. Many of the songs have been re-arranged in the book for flute/ recorder and guitar. Also included are many pages describing the life of Burns .

The Robert Burns Songbook for Guitar and Voice Vol 2

A second volume of 20 songs of Robert Burns arranged for guitar and voice. Full fingerstyle arrangements in notation and tablature, with chord symbols and detailed notes on all of the songs.

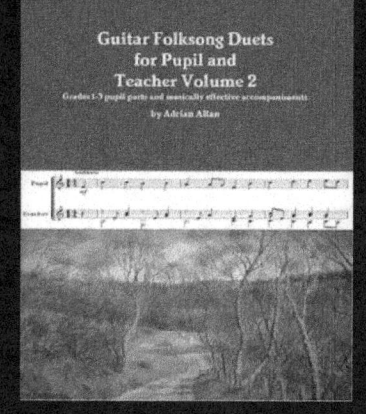

Guitar Folksong Duets Volume 2:

A second collection for pupil and teacher to play together. Includes: A Basque Lullaby; Beyond the Mountains; Early One Morning; Will Ye Go, Lassie; and many more

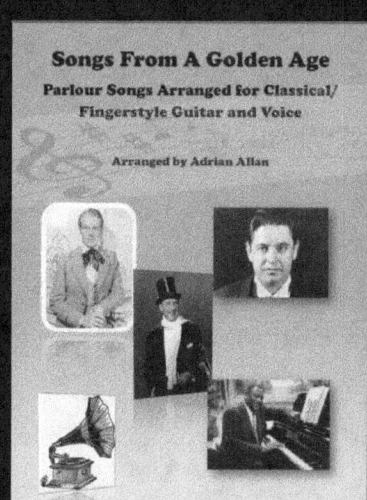

Popular Songs For Classical/ Fingerstyle Guitar

A collection of 21 intermediate arrangements for the classical or fingerstyle guitar in notation and tablature. The pieces are from the categories of Stephen Foster Songs; Folk Songs; Parlour Songs and arrangements of classical themes.

Songs from a Golden Age

8 fully professional arrangements of Victorian/Edwardian parlour songs arranged for the first time ever for guitar and medium voice

Including Trees, I Hear You Calling Me, Sylvia and many more

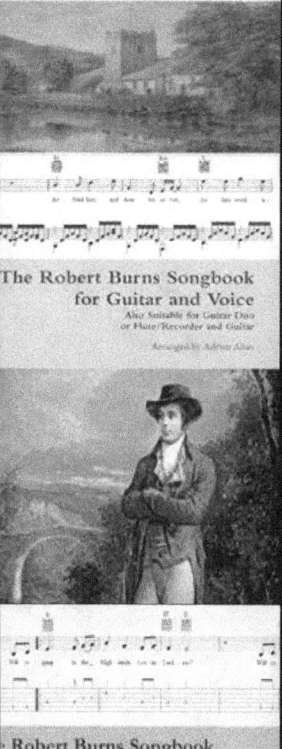

www.ingramcontent.com/pod-product-compliance
Lightning Source LLC
Chambersburg PA
CBHW081312180526
45170CB00007B/2674